BLOOM'S

HOW TO WRITE ABOUT

Mary Shelley

AMY WATKIN

BLOOM'S
LITERARY CRITICISM
An Infobase Learning Company

Bloom's How to Write about Mary Shelley

Bloom's Literary Criticism
An imprint of Infobase Learning
132 West 31st Street
New York NY 10001

Library of Congress Cataloging-in-Publication Data

Watkin, Amy
    Bloom's how to write about Mary Shelley / Amy Watkin ; Introduction by Harold Bloom.
        p. cm. — (Bloom's how to write about literature)
    Includes bibliographical references and index.
    ISBN 978-1-60413-748-4 (alk. paper)
    1. Shelley, Mary Wollstonecraft, 1797–1851—Criticism and interpretation. 2. Shelley, Mary Wollstonecraft, 1797–1851 Frankenstein. 3. Criticism—Authorship. 4. Report writing. I. Title. II. Title: How to write about Mary Shelley.
    PR5398.W38 2011
    823'.7—dc23

                                                                    2011031042

Chelsea House books are available at special discounts when purchased in bulk quantities for businesses, associations, institutions, or sales promotions. Please call our Special Sales Department in New York at (212) 967-8800 or (800) 322-8755.

You can find Bloom's Literary Criticism on the World Wide Web at
http://www.infobaselearning.com

Text design by Annie O'Donnell
Cover design by Ben Peterson
Composition by Erika K. Arroyo
Cover printed by Yurchak Printing, Landisville PA
Book printed and bound by Yurchak Printing, Landisville PA
Date printed: November 2011
Printed in the United States of America

10 9 8 7 6 5 4 3 2 1

All links and Web addresses were checked and verified to be correct at the time of publication. Because of the dynamic nature of the Web, some addresses and links may have changed since publication and may no longer be valid.

CONTENTS

SERIES
INTRODUCTION

BLOOM's How to Write about Literature series is designed to inspire students to write fine essays on great writers and their works. Each volume in the series begins with an introduction by Harold Bloom, meditating on the challenges and rewards of writing about the volume's subject author. The first chapter then provides detailed instructions on how to write a good essay, including how to find a thesis; how to develop an outline; how to write a good introduction, body text, and conclusion; how to cite sources; and more. The second chapter provides a brief overview of the issues involved in writing about the subject author and then a number of suggestions for paper topics, with accompanying strategies for addressing each topic. Succeeding chapters cover the author's major works.

The paper topics suggested within this book are open-ended, and the brief strategies provided are designed to give students a push forward in the writing process rather than a road map to success. The aim of the book is to pose questions, not answer them. Many different kinds of papers could result from each topic. As always, the success of each paper will depend completely on the writer's skill and imagination.

HOW TO WRITE ABOUT MARY SHELLEY: INTRODUCTION

by Harold Bloom

I HAVE, THROUGH the years, read all of Mary Shelley's fictions, but even *The Last Man* (1826) does not sustain rereading. Her first narrative, *Frankenstein* (1818), composed when she was nineteen, was to be her only canonical contribution to imaginative literature. The subtitle of *Frankenstein* is *The Modern Prometheus*, and the reader needs to remember that is the role of Victor Frankenstein. His achievement, the New Adam he had brought to life, ought not to be called the "monster" and perhaps even not the "creature." Think of him rather as the daimon first expounded by Empedocles. The daimon wandered through the cosmos, seeking to expiate previous incarnations with all their transgressions of bloodletting.

Victor Frankenstein's daimon is also his antithetical self, in a familiar romantic pattern that was to culminate in Nietzsche and in W.B. Yeats. Ironically, the daimon is both more intelligent and more passionate than his maker, with more capacity both for good and for evil. Compared to the daimon, Victor Frankenstein is a dreadful egomaniac, so solipsistic that he is incapable of understanding the moral enormity of what he has done. This crime is augmented when Frankenstein finds his creation abhorrent, rejects the daimon, and flees from him.

The poet Shelley, though he admired his wife's novel, necessarily was troubled by its implicit criticism of high romantic Byronic-Shelleyan Prometheanism. Young as she was, the daughter of William Godwin and Mary Wollstonecraft had inherited their radical vision of social realities and therefore resisted her husband's various transcendentalisms. Not that Victor Frankenstein was a portrait of Shelley; Clerval rather resembles the poet of *Prometheus Unbound*, and his murder by the daimon prompts my own uneasy reflections.

By any standard, Victor Frankenstein is a moral monster. We are moved by the daimon's pleas, but Frankenstein is not, even when they are eloquent with plangency:

> Oh, Frankenstein, be not equitable to every other, and trample upon me alone, to whom thy justice, and even thy clemency and affection, is most due. Remember that I am thy creature; *I ought to be thy Adam, but I am rather the fallen angel, whom thou drivest from joy for no misdeed.* Everywhere I see bliss, from which I alone am irrevocably excluded. I was benevolent and good; misery made me a fiend. Make me happy, and I shall again be virtuous.

The passage I italicize is the heart of the novel, deliberately recalling its epigraph from *Paradise Lost*, where the fallen Adam laments his creation:

> Did I request thee, Maker, from my clay
> To mold me man? Did I solicit thee
> From darkness to promote me?

Like the God of *Paradise Lost*, Victor Frankenstein manifests what I have to regard as moral idiocy:

> During these last days I have been occupied in examining my past conduct; nor do I find it blameable. In a fit of enthusiastic madness I created a rational creature, and was bound towards him, to assure, as far as was in my power, his happiness and well-being. This was my duty; but there was another still paramount to that. My duties towards the beings of my own species had greater claims to my attention, because they included a greater proportion of happiness or misery.

Peculiarly appalling, this self-revelation by the Modern Prometheus could not have been lost on the subtle and sensitive Shelley. We have debased the daimon in our ghastly series of filmed travesties called *Frankenstein*. For all his murderousness, the daimon remains the severe poet of the moral climate Mary Shelley created for him.

HOW TO WRITE
A GOOD ESSAY

By Laurie A. Sterling and Amy Watkin

WHILE THERE are many ways to write about literature, most assignments for high school and college English classes call for analytical papers. In these assignments, you are presenting your interpretation of a text to your reader. Your objective is to interpret the text's meaning in order to enhance your reader's understanding and enjoyment of the work. Without exception, strong papers about the meaning of a literary work are built upon a careful, close reading of the text or texts. Careful, analytical reading should always be the first step in your writing process. This volume provides models of such close, analytical reading, and these should help you develop your own skills as a reader and as a writer.

As the examples throughout this book demonstrate, attentive reading entails thinking about and evaluating the formal (textual) aspects of the author's works: theme, character, form, and language. In addition, when writing about a work, many readers choose to move beyond the text itself to consider the work's cultural context. In these instances, writers might explore the historical circumstances of the time period in which the work was written. Alternatively, they might examine the philosophies and ideas that a work addresses. Even in cases where writers explore a work's cultural context, though, papers must still address the more formal aspects of the work itself. A good interpretative essay that evaluates Charles Dickens's use of the philosophy of utilitarianism in his novel *Hard Times,* for example, cannot adequately address the author's treatment of the philosophy without firmly grounding this discussion in the book itself. In other words, any analytical paper about a text, even one that seeks to evaluate the work's cultural context, must also have a firm handle on the work's themes, characters, and language. You must look for and evaluate these aspects of a work, then, as you read a text and as you prepare to write about it.

WRITING ABOUT THEMES

Literary themes are more than just topics or subjects treated in a work; they are attitudes or points about these topics that often structure other elements in a work. Writing about theme therefore requires that you not just identify a topic that a literary work addresses but also discuss what the work says about that topic. For example, if you were writing about the culture of the American South in William Faulkner's famous story "A Rose for Emily," you would need to discuss what Faulkner says, argues, or implies about that culture and its passing.

When you prepare to write about thematic concerns in a work of literature, you will probably discover that, like most works of literature, your text touches upon other themes in addition to its central theme. These secondary themes also provide rich ground for paper topics. A thematic paper on "A Rose for Emily" might consider gender or race in the story. While neither of these could be said to be the central theme of the story, they are clearly related to the passing of the "old South" and could provide plenty of good material for papers.

As you prepare to write about themes in literature, you might find a number of strategies helpful. After you identify a theme or themes in the story, you should begin by evaluating how other elements of the story—such as character, point of view, imagery, and symbolism—help develop the theme. You might ask yourself what your own responses are to the author's treatment of the subject matter. Do not neglect the obvious, either: What expectations does the title set up? How does the title help develop thematic concerns? Clearly, the title "A Rose for Emily" says something about the narrator's attitude toward the title character, Emily Grierson, and all she represents.

WRITING ABOUT CHARACTER

Generally, characters are essential components of fiction and drama. (This is not always the case, though; Ray Bradbury's "August 2026: There Will Come Soft Rains" is technically a story without characters, at least any human characters.) Often, you can discuss character in poetry, as in T. S. Eliot's "The Love Song of J. Alfred Prufrock" or Robert Browning's "My Last Duchess." Many writers find that analyzing character is one of the most interesting and engaging ways to work with a piece of literature and to shape a paper. After all, characters generally are human, and we all know something about being human and living in the world. While it is always important to remember that these figures are not real people but creations of the writer's imagination, it can be fruitful to begin evaluating them as you might evaluate a real person. Often you can start with your own response to a character. Did you like or dislike the character? Did you sympathize with the character? Why or why not?

Keep in mind, though, that emotional responses like these are just starting places. To truly explore and evaluate literary characters, you need to return to the formal aspects of the text and evaluate how the author has drawn these characters. The 20th-century writer E. M. Forster coined the terms *flat* characters and *round* characters. Flat characters are static, one-dimensional characters that frequently represent a particular concept or idea. In contrast, round characters are fully drawn and much more realistic characters that frequently change and develop over the course of a work. Are the characters you are studying flat or round? What elements of the characters lead you to this conclusion? Why might the author have drawn characters like this? How does their development affect the meaning of the work? Similarly, you should explore the techniques the author uses to develop characters. Do we hear a character's own words, or do we hear only other characters' assessments of him or her? Or, does the author use an omniscient or limited omniscient narrator to allow us access to the workings of the characters' minds? If so, how does that help develop the characterization? Often you can even evaluate the narrator as a character. How trustworthy are the opinions and assessments of the narrator? You should also think about characters' names. Do they mean anything? If you encounter a hero named Sophia or Sophie, you should probably think about her wisdom (or lack thereof), since *sophia* means "wisdom" in Greek. Similarly, since the name Sylvia is derived from the word *sylvan,* meaning "of the wood," you might want to evaluate that character's relationship with nature. Once again, you might look to the title of the work. Does Herman Melville's "Bartleby, the Scrivener" signal anything about Bartleby himself? Is Bartleby adequately defined by his job as scrivener? Is this part of Melville's point? Pursuing questions such as these can help you develop thorough papers about characters from psychological, sociological, or more formalistic perspectives.

WRITING ABOUT FORM AND GENRE

Genre, a word derived from French, means "type" or "class." Literary genres are distinctive classes or categories of literary composition. On the most general level, literary works can be divided into the genres of drama, poetry, fiction, and essays, yet within those genres there are classifications that are also referred to as genres. Tragedy and comedy, for example, are genres of drama. Epic, lyric, and pastoral are genres of poetry. *Form,* on the other hand, generally refers to the shape or structure of a work. There are many clearly defined forms of poetry that follow specific patterns of meter, rhyme, and stanza. Sonnets, for example, are poems that follow a fixed form of 14 lines. Sonnets generally follow one of two basic sonnet forms, each with its own distinct rhyme scheme. Haiku is another example of poetic form, traditionally consisting of three unrhymed lines of five, seven, and five syllables.

While you might think that writing about form or genre might leave little room for argument, many of these forms and genres are very fluid. Remember that literature is evolving and ever changing, and so are its forms. As you study poetry, you may find that poets, especially more modern poets, play with traditional poetic forms, bringing about new effects. Similarly, dramatic tragedy was once quite narrowly defined, but over the centuries playwrights have broadened and challenged traditional definitions, changing the shape of tragedy. When Arthur Miller wrote *Death of a Salesman,* many critics challenged the idea that tragic drama could encompass a common man like Willy Loman.

Evaluating how a work of literature fits into or challenges the bound-aries of its form or genre can provide you with fruitful avenues of inves-tigation. You might find it helpful to ask why the work does or does not fit into traditional categories. Why might Miller have thought it fitting to write a tragedy of the common man? Similarly, you might compare the content or theme of a work with its form. How well do they work together? Many of Emily Dickinson's poems, for instance, follow the meter of traditional hymns. While some of her poems seem to express traditional religious doctrines, many seem to challenge or strain against traditional conceptions of God and theology. What is the effect, then, of her use of traditional hymn meter?

WRITING ABOUT LANGUAGE, SYMBOLS, AND IMAGERY

No matter what the genre, writers use words as their most basic tool. Lan-guage is the most fundamental building block of literature. It is essential that you pay careful attention to the author's language and word choice as you read, reread, and analyze a text. Imagery is language that appeals to the senses. Most commonly, imagery appeals to our sense of vision, cre-ating a mental picture, but authors also use language that appeals to our other senses. Images can be literal or figurative. Literal images use sensory language to describe an actual thing. In the broadest terms, figurative lan-guage uses one thing to speak about something else. For example, if I call my boss a snake, I am not saying that he is literally a reptile. Instead, I am using figurative language to communicate my opinions about him. Since we think of snakes as sneaky, slimy, and sinister, I am using the concrete image of a snake to communicate these abstract opinions and impressions.

The two most common figures of speech are similes and metaphors. Both are comparisons between two apparently dissimilar things. Simi-les are explicit comparisons using the words *like* or *as*; metaphors are implicit comparisons. To return to the previous example, if I say, "My boss, Bob, was waiting for me when I showed up to work five minutes late today—the snake!" I have constructed a metaphor. Writing about his experiences fighting in World War I, Wilfred Owen begins his poem "Dulce et decorum est" with a string of similes: "Bent double, like old beg-gars under sacks, / Knock-kneed, coughing like hags, we cursed through sludge." Owen's goal was to undercut clichéd notions that war and dying in battle were glorious. Certainly, comparing soldiers to coughing hags and to beggars underscores his point.

"Fog," a short poem by Carl Sandburg, provides a clear example of a metaphor. Sandburg's poem reads:

> The fog comes
> on little cat feet.
>
> It sits looking
> over harbor and city
> on silent haunches
> and then moves on.

Notice how effectively Sandburg conveys surprising impressions of the fog by comparing two seemingly disparate things—the fog and a cat.

Symbols, by contrast, are things that stand for, or represent, other things. Often they represent something intangible, such as concepts or ideas. In everyday life we use and understand symbols easily. Babies at christenings and brides at weddings wear white to represent purity. Think, too, of a dollar bill. The paper itself has no value in and of itself. Instead, that paper bill is a symbol of something else, the precious metal in a nation's coffers. Symbols in literature work similarly. Authors use symbols to evoke more than a simple, straightforward, literal meaning. Characters, objects, and places can all function as symbols. Famous literary examples of symbols include Moby Dick, the white whale of Herman Melville's novel, and the scarlet *A* of Nathaniel Hawthorne's *The Scarlet Letter*. As both of these symbols suggest, a literary symbol cannot be adequately defined or explained by any one meaning. Hester Prynne's Puritan community clearly intends her scarlet *A* as a symbol of her adultery, but as the novel progresses, even her own community reads the letter as representing not just *adultery*, but *able, angel*, and a host of other meanings.

Writing about imagery and symbols requires close attention to the author's language. To prepare a paper on symbolism or imagery in a work, identify and trace the images and symbols and then try to draw some conclusions about how they function. Ask yourself how any symbols or images help contribute to the themes or meanings of the work. What connotations do they carry? How do they affect your reception of the work? Do they shed light on characters or settings? A strong paper on imagery or symbolism will thoroughly consider the use of figures in the text and will try to reach some conclusions about how or why the author uses them.

WRITING ABOUT HISTORY AND CONTEXT

As noted above, it is possible to write an analytical paper that also considers the work's context. After all, the text was not created in a vacuum. The author lived and wrote in a specific time period and in a specific cultural context and, like all of us, was shaped by that environment. Learning more about the historical and cultural circumstances that surround the author and the work can help illuminate a text and provide you with productive material for a paper. Remember, though, that when you write analytical papers, you should use the context to illuminate the text. Do not lose sight of your goal—to interpret the meaning of the literary work. Use historical or philosophical research as a tool to develop your textual evaluation.

Thoughtful readers often consider how history and culture affected the author's choice and treatment of his or her subject matter. Investigations into the history and context of a work could examine the work's relation to specific historical events, such as the Salem witch trials in seventeenth-century Massachusetts or the restoration of Charles II to the English throne in 1660. Bear in mind that historical context is not limited to politics and world events. While knowing about the Vietnam War is certainly helpful in interpreting much of Tim O'Brien's fiction, and some knowledge of the French Revolution clearly illuminates the dynamics of Charles Dickens's *A Tale of Two Cities*, historical context also entails the fabric of daily life. Examining a text in light of gender roles, race relations, class boundaries, or working conditions can give rise to thoughtful and compelling papers. Exploring the conditions of the working class in nineteenth-century England, for example, can provide a particularly effective avenue for writing about Dickens's *Hard Times*.

You can begin thinking about these issues by asking broad questions at first. What do you know about the time period and about the author? What does the editorial apparatus in your text tell you? Similarly, when specific historical events or dynamics are particularly important to understanding a work but might be somewhat obscure to modern readers, textbooks usually provide notes to explain historical background. With this information, ask yourself how these historical facts and circumstances might have affected the author, the presentation of theme, and the presentation of character. How does knowing more about the work's specific historical context illuminate the work? To take a well-known example, understanding the complex attitudes toward slavery during the time Mark Twain wrote *Adventures of Huckleberry Finn* should help you begin to examine issues of race in the text. Additionally, you might compare these attitudes to those of the time in which the novel was set. How might this comparison affect your interpretation of a work written after the abolition of slavery but set before the Civil War?

WRITING ABOUT PHILOSOPHY AND IDEAS

Philosophical concerns are closely related to both historical context and thematic issues. Like historical investigation, philosophical research can provide a useful tool as you analyze a text. For example, an investigation into the working class in Dickens's England might lead you to a topic on the philosophical doctrine of utilitarianism in *Hard Times*. Many other works explore philosophies and ideas quite explicitly. Mary Shelley's famous novel *Frankenstein*, for example, explores John Locke's tabula rasa theory of human knowledge as she portrays the intellectual and emotional development of Victor Frankenstein's creature. As this example indicates, philosophical issues are more abstract than investigations of theme or historical context. Some other examples of philosophical issues include human free will, the formation of human identity, the nature of sin, or questions of ethics.

Writing about philosophy and ideas might require some outside research, but usually the notes or other material in your text will provide you with basic information, and often footnotes and bibliographies suggest places you can go to read further about the subject. If you have identified a philosophical theme that runs through a text, you might ask yourself how the author develops this theme. Look at character development and the interactions of characters, for example. Similarly, you might examine whether the narrative voice in a work of fiction addresses the philosophical concerns of the text.

WRITING COMPARISON AND CONTRAST ESSAYS

Finally, you might find that comparing and contrasting the works or techniques of an author provides a useful tool for literary analysis. A comparison and contrast essay might compare two characters or themes in a single work, or it might compare the author's treatment of a theme in two works. It might also contrast methods of character development or analyze an author's differing treatment of a philosophical concern in two works. Writing comparison and contrast essays, though, requires some special consideration. While they generally provide you with plenty of material to use, they also come with a built-in trap: the laundry list. These papers often become mere lists of connections between the works. As this chapter will discuss, a strong thesis must make an assertion that you want to prove or validate. A strong comparison/contrast thesis, then, needs to comment on the significance of the similarities and differences you observe. It is not enough merely to assert that the works contain similarities and differences. You might, for example, assert why the similarities and differences are important and explain how they illuminate the works' treatment of theme. Remember, too, that a thesis should not be a statement of the obvious. A comparison/contrast paper that focuses only on very obvious similarities or differences does little to illuminate the connections between the works. Often, an effective method of shaping a strong thesis and argument is to begin your paper by noting the similarities between the works but then to develop a thesis that asserts how these apparently similar elements are different. If, for example, you observe that Emily Dickinson wrote a number of poems about spiders, you might analyze how she uses spider imagery differently in two poems. Similarly, many scholars have noted that Hawthorne created many "mad scientist" characters, men who are so devoted to their science or their art that they lose perspective on all else. A good thesis comparing two of these characters—Aylmer of "The Birth-mark" and Dr. Rappaccini of "Rappaccini's Daughter," for example—might initially identify both characters as examples of Hawthorne's mad scientist type but then argue that their motivations for scientific experimentation differ. If you strive to analyze the similarities or differences, discuss significances, and move beyond the obvious, your paper should move beyond the laundry list trap.

PREPARING TO WRITE

Armed with a clear sense of your task—illuminating the text—and with an understanding of theme, character, language, history, and philosophy, you are ready to approach the writing process. Remember that good writing is grounded in good reading and that close reading takes time, attention, and more than one reading of your text. Read for comprehension first. As you go back and review the work, mark the text to chart the details of the work as well as your reactions. Highlight important passages, repeated words, and image patterns. "Converse" with the text through marginal notes. Mark turns in the plot, ask questions, and make observations about characters, themes, and language. If you are reading from a book that does not belong to you, keep a record of your reactions in a journal or notebook. If you have read a work of literature carefully, paying attention to both the text and the context of the work, you have a leg up on the writing process. Admittedly, at this point, your ideas are probably very broad and undefined, but you have taken an important first step toward writing a strong paper.

Your next step is to focus, to take a broad, perhaps fuzzy, topic and define it more clearly. Even a topic provided by your instructor will need to be focused appropriately. Remember that good writers make the topic their own. There are a number of strategies—often called "invention"—that you can use to develop your own focus. In one such strategy, called *freewriting*, you spend 10 minutes or so just writing about your topic without referring back to the text or your notes. Write whatever comes to mind; the important thing is that you just keep writing. Often this process allows you to develop fresh ideas or approaches to your subject matter. You could also try *brainstorming*: Write down your topic and then list all the related points or ideas you can think of. Include questions, comments, words, important passages or events, and anything else that comes to mind. Let one idea lead to another. In the related technique of *clustering*, or *mapping*, write your topic on a sheet of paper and write related ideas around it. Then list related subpoints under each of these main ideas. Many people then draw arrows to show connections between points. This technique helps you narrow your topic and can also help you organize your ideas. Similarly, asking journalistic questions— Who? What? Where? When? Why? and How?—can lead to ideas for topic development.

Thesis Statements

Once you have developed a focused topic, you can begin to think about your thesis statement, the main point or purpose of your paper. It is imperative that you craft a strong thesis, otherwise, your paper will likely be little more than random, disorganized observations about the text. Think of your thesis statement as a kind of road map for your paper. It tells your reader where you are going and how you are going to get there.

To craft a good thesis, you must keep a number of things in mind. First, as the title of this subsection indicates, your paper's thesis should be a statement, an assertion about the text that you want to prove or validate. Beginning writers often formulate a question that they attempt to use as a thesis. For example, a writer exploring the theme of gender in Shelley's *Frankenstein* might ask, What role does gender play in this novel? While a question like this is a good strategy to use in the invention process to help narrow your topic and find your thesis, it cannot serve as the thesis statement because it does not tell your reader what you want to assert about gender. You might shape this question into a thesis by instead proposing an answer to that question: While it can be said that the males in *Frankenstein* embody female voices through the inherent fact that they are written by a woman, through their very masculine flaws and actions, the male characters support and uphold the importance of the female role in society. Notice that this thesis provides an initial plan or structure for the rest of the paper, and please note that the thesis statement does not necessarily have to fit into one sentence. After discussing gender, you could examine the ways in which gender is presented as problematic in this novel and then theorize about what Shelley is saying about gender more generally.

Second, remember that a good thesis makes an assertion that you need to support. In other words, a good thesis does not state the obvious. If you tried to formulate a thesis about gender by simply saying, Gender is important in *Frankenstein,* you have done nothing but rephrase the obvious. Since Shelley's novel is written by a woman with main male characters and several important females, there would be no point in spending three to five pages supporting that assertion. You might try to develop a thesis from that point by asking yourself some further questions: What does it mean when any given character implies that women are merely decorative? Does the play seem to indicate that women and men are unequal in most ways? Does it present womanhood as an advantage in this world, or is womanhood presented as a source of vulnerability? Can some of the issues surrounding gender in the novel be attributed to other factors, such as class? Such a line of questioning might lead you to a more viable thesis, like the one in the preceding paragraph.

As the comparison with the road map also suggests, your thesis should appear near the beginning of the paper. In relatively short papers (three to six pages) the thesis almost always appears in the first para-graph. Some writers fall into the trap of saving their thesis for the end, trying to provide a surprise or a big moment of revelation, as if to say, "TA-DA! I've just proved that in *Frankenstein* Shelley uses darkness to symbolize Frankenstein's true character." Placing a thesis at the end of an essay can seriously mar the essay's effectiveness. If you fail to define your essay's point and purpose clearly at the beginning, your reader will find it difficult to assess the clarity of your argument and understand the points you are making. When your argument comes as a surprise at the end, you force your reader to reread your essay in order to assess its logic and effectiveness.

Finally, you should avoid using the first person ("I") as you present your thesis. Though it is not strictly wrong to write in the first person, it is diffi-cult to do so gracefully. While writing in the first person, beginning writ-ers often fall into the trap of writing self-reflexive prose (writing *about* their paper *in* their paper). Often this leads to the most dreaded of open-ing lines: In this paper I am going to discuss. . . . Not only does this self-reflexive voice make for awkward prose, but it frequently allows writers to boldly announce a topic while completely avoiding a the-sis statement. An example might be a paper that begins as follows: Mary Shelley's *Frankenstein* takes place at the beginning of the Industrial Revolution as science was emerging in new ways. In this paper I am going to discuss how the women in the novel react to this. The author of this paper has done little more than announce a general topic for the paper (the reaction of women to cultural/societal changes). While the last sentence might be a thesis, the writer fails to present an opinion about the significance of the reaction. To improve this "thesis," the writer would need to back up a couple of steps. First, the announced topic of the paper is too broad; it largely summarizes the events in the story, without saying anything about the ideas in the story. The writer should highlight what she considers the meaning of the story: What is the story about? The writer might conclude that the major societal and cultural changes create feelings of inadequacy in the women. From here, the author could select the means by which Shelley communicates these ideas and then begin to craft a specific thesis. A writer who chooses to explore the impact of science on women at the beginning of the nineteenth century, for example, craft a thesis that reads, In *Frankenstein*, Mary Shelley's women warn the male characters of the dangerous direction in which science and industry are headed at the beginning of the nineteenth century.

Outlines

While developing a strong, thoughtful thesis early in your writing process should help focus your paper, outlining provides an essential tool for logically shaping that paper. A good outline helps you see—and develop—the relationships among the points in your argument and assures you that your paper flows logically and coherently. Outlining not only helps place your points in a logical order but also helps you subordinate supporting points, weed out any irrelevant points, and decide if there are any necessary points that are missing from your argument. Most of us are familiar with formal outlines that use numerical and letter designations for each point. However, there are different types of outlines; you may find that an informal outline is a more useful tool for you. What is important, though, is that you spend the time to develop some sort of outline—formal or informal.

Remember that an outline is a tool to help you shape and write a strong paper. If you do not spend sufficient time planning your supporting points and shaping the arrangement of those points, you will most likely construct a vague, unfocused outline that provides little, if any, help with the writing of the paper. Consider the following example.

Thesis: While it can be said that the males in *Frankenstein* embody female voices through the inherent fact that they are written by a woman, through their very masculine flaws and actions, they support and uphold the importance of the female role in society.

I. Introduction and thesis

II. Male ignorance
    A. Frankenstein

III. Walton

IV. *Paradise Lost*

V. Phasing out the female
    A. Happiness
    B. Partnership
    C. Undeveloped characters
    D. The creature

VI. Conclusion
    A. Showing that women are powerful by effects rather than direct reason, Shelley is using intelligence and cleverness to demonstrate that males may not be as superior to females as they may expect.

This outline has a number of flaws. First, the major topics labeled with the roman numerals are not arranged in a logical order. If the paper's focus is on phasing out the female, the writer should establish the particulars of that concept before showing how male ignorance plays a role in gendered situations. Similarly, the thesis makes no reference to *Paradise Lost*, but the writer includes the title as a major section of this outline. The writer could, however, include *Paradise Lost* in terms of its influence on the creature's concept of relationships/gender. As one of the main male char-acters in the novel, Walton may well have a place in this paper, but the writer fails to provide details about his place in the argument. Third, the writer includes the creature's character as one of the lettered items in section V. Letters A, B, and C all refer to specific instances where the concept of phasing out the female will be discussed; the creature does not appear to belong in this list. A fourth problem is the inclusion of a section A in section II. An outline should not include an A without a B, a 1 without a 2, and so forth. The final problem with this outline is the overall lack of detail. None of the sections provide much information about the content of the argument, and it seems likely that the writer has not given sufficient thought to the content of the paper.

A better start to this outline might be the following:

Thesis: While it can be said that the males in *Frankenstein* embody female voices through the inherent fact that they are written by a woman, through their very masculine flaws and actions, they support and uphold the importance of the female role in society.

I. Introduction and thesis

II. Relationships with women
    A. Walton
    B. Frankenstein
    C. The creature

III. Woman as complementary partner
    A. Elizabeth
    B. Walton's sister

IV. Usurpation of woman's role in reproduction
    A. Role of female and art
    B. The second creature

V. Shelley's role as writer
    A. Philosophies
    B. Intentions

```
VI. Conclusion
    A. Showing that women are powerful by effects
    rather than direct reason, Shelley is using
    intelligence and cleverness to demonstrate
    that males may not be as superior to females
    as they may expect.
```

This new outline would prove much more helpful when it came time to write the paper.

An outline like this could be shaped into an even more useful tool if the writer fleshed out the argument by providing specific examples from the text to support each point. Once you have listed your main point and your supporting ideas, develop this raw material by listing related supporting ideas and material under each of those main headings. From there, arrange the material in subsections and order the material logically.

For example, you might begin with one of the theses cited above: While it can be said that the males in *Frankenstein* embody female voices through the inherent fact that they are written by a woman, through their very masculine flaws and actions, they support and uphold the importance of the female role in society. As noted above, this thesis already gives you the beginning of an organization: Start by providing the necessary background about male ignorance and then explain how Shelley presents her male characters at least partly in order to emphasize the importance of women. You might begin your outline, then, with four topic headings: (1) examine males' ignorance, (2) relationships with women, (3) women as complementary partners, and (4) how such information influences our understanding of Shelley's intentions. Under each of those headings you could list ideas that support the particular point. Be sure to include references to parts of the text that help build your case.

An informal outline might look like this:

```
Thesis: While it can be said that the males in
Frankenstein embody female voices through the inherent
fact that they are written by a woman, through their
```

very masculine flaws and actions, they support and uphold the importance of the female role in society.

1. Examine males' ignorance
   • Demanding a woman as complementary partner
   • Usurpation of woman's role in reproduction

2. Relationships with women
   • All males with or in search of female partner
   • Connection to maturity

3. Woman as complementary partner
   • Elizabeth: "if I see but one smile on your lips when we meet . . . I shall need no other happiness" (Shelley 130)
   • Elizabeth's role as literary function, not character: " 'little happiness remains for us on earth; yet all that I may one day enjoy is concentered [sic] in you' " (Shelley 131)
   • Creature wants female companion
   • Autobiographical tone of novel: "a text frequently read as a critical portrait of Percy" (London 255)
   • Role of female and art
   • Disastrous results with only men involved

4. Shelley's role as writer
   • Role of female in art
   • Intentions

5. Conclusion
   Showing that women are powerful by effects rather than direct reason, Shelley is using intelligence and cleverness to demonstrate that males may not be as superior to females as they may expect.

You would set about writing a formal outline with a similar process, though in the final stages you would label the headings differently. A formal outline for a paper that argues the thesis about *Frankenstein* cited above—that the preponderance of male characters in the novel actually supports the importance of women—might look like this:

Thesis: While it can be said that the males in *Frankenstein* embody female voices through the inherent fact that they are written by a woman, through their very masculine flaws and actions, they support and uphold the importance of the female role in society.

I. Introduction and thesis

II. Examining males' ignorance
    1. Walton and his sister
    2. Frankenstein and Elizabeth
    3. The creature, his reading, and his need for a partner

III. Woman as complementary partner
    1. Male characters striving for maturity
    2. Domestic healing of pain from absent mothers
    3. Elizabeth's role as literary function, not character
    4. Creature wants female companion

IV. Usurpation of women's role in reproduction
    1. Disastrous results with only men involved
    2. Creation of the female monster

V. How such information influences our understanding of Shelley's intentions
    1. Autobiographical tone of novel: "a text frequently read as a critical portrait of Percy" (London 255)
    2. Role of female and art

VI. Conclusion

> By examining the vices and follies of the
> men in *Frankenstein*, it is demonstrated
> that, while it may be a male-character-
> driven novel, the powerful voice of women,
> and the helm of its authoress, are still
> highly prevalent. Showing that women are
> powerful by effects rather than direct
> reason, Shelley is using intelligence and
> cleverness to demonstrate that males may
> not be as superior to females as they may
> expect.

As in the previous example outline, the thesis provided the seeds of a structure, and the writer was careful to arrange the supporting points in a logical manner, showing the relationships among the ideas in the paper.

Body Paragraphs

Once your outline is complete, you can begin drafting your paper. Paragraphs, units of related sentences, are the building blocks of a good paper, and as you draft you should keep in mind both the function and the qualities of good paragraphs. Paragraphs help you chart and control the shape and content of your essay, and they help the reader see your organization and your logic. You should begin a new paragraph whenever you move from one major point to another. In longer, more complex essays you might use a group of related paragraphs to support major points. Remember that in addition to being adequately developed, a good paragraph is both unified and coherent.

Unified Paragraphs

Each paragraph must be centered around one idea or point, and a unified paragraph carefully focuses on and develops this central idea without including extraneous ideas or tangents. For beginning writers, the best way to ensure that you are constructing unified paragraphs is to include a topic sentence in each paragraph. This topic sentence should convey the main point of the paragraph, and every sentence in the paragraph should relate to that topic sentence. Any sentence that strays from the central topic does not belong in the paragraph and needs to be revised or deleted. Consider the following paragraph about the search for female partners in *Frankenstein*. Notice how the paragraph veers away from the main point that these searches reinforce the importance of women in the novel:

> The three distinct male characters that the readers are introduced to at the beginning of the novel are Walton, Frankenstein, and for all intents and purposes the creature, or at least the idea of the masculine creature is introduced. All of these males have some sort of female partner or are in search of a female partner. Mary Poovey describes this need as the male characters wanting to reach maturity: "[Shelley] continues to dramatize personal fulfillment . . . with the absent mother being replaced by the closest female equivalent . . . the beloved object would be sought and found only within the comforting confines of preexistent domestic relationships" (Poovey 335). James Wohlpart argues that Shelley writes in a time when literature was dominated by males, and as such, most of the creation, so to speak, fell within the hands of the males, and it bypassed the females: "[Shelley] also implicates the tradition which led up this period, suggesting that artistic creativity has predominately become . . . a male pursuit" (Wohlpart 266). Thus Shelley takes back the role of the female in art and demonstrates that one cannot have art and beauty without a woman. In short, nothing can be produced without a woman being involved in some way, shape, or form. Thus when Frankenstein attempts to do just that, the disastrous results that occur prove the wrong that has been done by trying to create life with only male entities.

Although the paragraph begins solidly, and the first sentence provides the central idea of the paragraph, the author soon goes on a tangent. If the purpose of the paragraph is to demonstrate that the search for female partners plays an integral role in the novel, the sentences about Shelley as a writer are tangential here. They may find a place later in the paper, but they should be deleted from this paragraph.

Coherent Paragraphs

In addition to shaping unified paragraphs, you must also craft coherent paragraphs, paragraphs that develop their points logically with sentences that flow smoothly into one another. Coherence depends on the order of your sentences, but it is not strictly the order of the sentences that is important to paragraph coherence. You also need to craft your prose to help the reader see the relationship among the sentences.

Consider the following paragraph about the search for female partners in *Frankenstein*. Notice how the writer uses the same ideas as the paragraph above yet fails to help the reader see the relationships among the points.

> The three distinct male characters that the readers are introduced to at the beginning of the novel are Walton, Frankenstein, and the creature—or at least the idea of the masculine creature. All of these males have some sort of female partner or are in search of a female partner. The men need to fully fulfill themselves by finding a companion, but not just any companion, one that domestically would help heal them from the pain of an absent mother. Walton has found his "more than sister" in Mrs. Saville and addresses and signs the letters in a way that suggests that their bond is uncommonly strong.

This paragraph demonstrates that unity alone does not guarantee paragraph effectiveness. The argument is hard to follow because the author fails both to show connections between the sentences and to indicate how they work to support the overall point.

A number of techniques are available to aid paragraph coherence. Careful use of transitional words and phrases is essential. You can use transitional flags to introduce an example or an illustration *(for example, for instance),* to amplify a point or add another phase of the same idea *(additionally, furthermore, next, similarly, finally, then),* to indicate a conclusion or result *(therefore, as a result, thus, in other words),* to signal a contrast or a qualification *(on the other hand, nevertheless, despite this, on the contrary, still, however, conversely)*, to signal a comparison *(likewise, in comparison, similarly)*, and to indicate a movement in time *(afterward, earlier, eventually, finally, later, subsequently, until)*.

In addition to transitional flags, careful use of pronouns aids coherence and flow. If you were writing about *The Wizard of Oz*, you would not want to keep repeating the phrase *the witch* or the name *Dorothy*. Careful substitution of the pronoun *she* in these instances can aid coherence. A word of warning, though: When you substitute pronouns for proper names, always be sure that your pronoun reference is clear. In a paragraph that discusses both Dorothy and the witch, substituting *she* could lead to confusion. Make sure that it is clear to whom the pronoun refers. Generally, the pronoun refers to the last proper noun you have used.

While repeating the same name over and over again can lead to awkward, boring prose, it is possible to use repetition to help your paragraph's coherence. Careful repetition of important words or phrases can lend coherence to your paragraph by reminding readers of your key points. Admittedly, it takes some practice to use this technique effectively. You may find that reading your prose aloud can help you develop an ear for effective use of repetition.

To see how helpful transitional aids are, compare the paragraph below to the preceding paragraph about the search for female partners in *Frankenstein*. Notice how the author works with the same ideas and quotations but shapes them into a much more coherent paragraph whose point is clearer and easier to follow.

> The three distinct male characters that the readers
> are introduced to at the beginning of the novel are
> Walton, Frankenstein, and the creature—or at least the
> idea of the masculine creature. All of these males
> have some sort of female partner or are in search of a
> female partner. Mary Poovey describes this need as the
> male characters wanting to reach maturity: "[Shelley]
> continues to dramatize personal fulfillment . . . with
> the absent mother being replaced by the closest female
> equivalent . . . the beloved object would be sought and

found only within the comforting confines of preexistent domestic relationships" (Poovey 335). With this in mind then, it seems that the men need to fully fulfill themselves by finding a companion, but not just any companion—one that domestically would help heal them from the pain of an absent mother. Through this, the males choose women who are familial but, as literary characters, appear only to serve as a function. Walton has found his "more than sister" in Mrs. Saville and addresses and signs the letters in a way that suggest that their bond is uncommonly strong: "I love you tenderly . . . remember me with affection" (Shelley 12). He uses his sister as a vessel to tell the story and uses her as a springboard to give him comfort, though not once are we given any inclination as to the character of Mrs. Saville herself. She remains an empty canvas, a theme that can also be conveyed in Victor's "more than sister," Elizabeth Larenza.

Similarly, the following paragraph demonstrates both unity and coherence. In it, the author argues that Elizabeth's role may be as literary function rather than fully rounded character.

Elizabeth is declared to be Victor's mate, and Victor acknowledges this without actually knowing how she feels about the match. It was his mother's dying wish, and rather than pursue the courting facet of the relationship, both characters assume the wish as fact. Toward the end of the novel, in a letter that Elizabeth writes to Victor, we are presented with her feelings, "if I see but one smile on your lips when we meet . . . I shall need no other happiness" (Shelley 130), but these seem to come rather unsupported. We understand through this letter that Elizabeth loves Victor, but the events or feelings that led to this are absent, furthering the argument that Elizabeth's role in the novel is as a literary function, not as a character. All

that is important is that Elizabeth is meant for Victor,
and Victor depends on Elizabeth for his happiness,
especially after his multiple confrontations with the
creature.

Introductions

Introductions present particular challenges for writers. Generally, your introduction should do two things: capture your reader's attention and explain the main point of your essay. In other words, while your introduction should contain your thesis, it needs to do a bit more work than that. You are likely to find that starting that first paragraph is one of the most difficult parts of the paper. It is hard to face that blank page or screen, and as a result, many beginning writers, in desperation to start somewhere, start with overly broad, general statements. While it is often a good strategy to start with more general subject matter and narrow your focus, do not begin with broad sweeping statements such as, Everyone likes to be creative and feel understood. Such sentences are nothing but empty filler. They begin to fill the blank page, but they do nothing to advance your argument. Instead, you should try to gain your readers' interest. Some writers like to begin with a pertinent quotation or with a relevant question. Or, you might begin with an introduction of the topic you will discuss. If you are writing about Shelley's presentation of male characters, for instance, you might begin by talking about those characters' perspectives. Another common trap to avoid is depending on your title to introduce the author and the text you are writing about. Always include the work's author and title in your opening paragraph.

Compare the effectiveness of the following introductions.

1.
Throughout history, women have been oppressed. Think
how you feel when you really want something: It makes
you feel bad when you don't get it, right? In this
story, Shelley shows characters' different points of
view about women. More importantly, she shows how women
function.

2.

If asked to find a novel that clearly illustrated the superiority of the male sex, some might naïvely point to Mary Shelley's *Frankenstein*. Upfront we see a tale dominated by male characters; in fact, the few females that are present embody rather vacant personas, serving as functions rather than as people. However, when one considers the role of females in the grand scheme of the novel, we are able to understand the importance of the female to the work overall as well as in the theme that Shelley is conveying. While it can be said that the males in *Frankenstein* embody female voices through the inherent fact that they are written by a woman, through their very masculine flaws and actions, the male characters support and uphold the importance of the female role in society. By insisting that the woman only serves as a function, that function becomes more relevant as the male figures try to phase females out of the story altogether. Thus *Frankenstein* becomes a cautionary tale of what happens when men try to live without women, and clearly it has disastrous results.

The first introduction begins with a vague, overly broad sentence; cites unclear, undeveloped examples; and then moves abruptly to the very weak thesis. Notice, too, how a reader deprived of the paper's title does not know the title of the story that the paper will analyze. The second introduction works with the same material and thesis but provides more detail and is consequently much more interesting. It begins by discussing significance of gender in characterizations, briefly mentions a theme in the novel, and then gives specific examples. The paragraph ends with the thesis. This effective introduction also includes the title of the text and full name of the author.

The paragraph below provides another example of an opening strategy. It begins by introducing the author and the text it will analyze, and then it moves on by briefly introducing relevant details of the story in order to set up its thesis.

Mary Shelley's novel, *Frankenstein*, centers on Victor Frankenstein and the creature, two male characters doing their best to find female partners. Shelley's ideas about gender in the early nineteenth century come through rather unexpectedly, since most readers do not consider *Frankenstein* a novel much concerned with gender issues. What Shelley does in this novel is surprise readers by using female characters like Elizabeth as vehicles for emphasizing a particular point about the role of women.

Conclusions

Conclusions present another series of challenges for writers. No doubt you have heard the adage about writing papers: "Tell us what you are going to say, say it, and then tell us what you've said." While this formula does not necessarily result in bad papers, it does not often result in good ones, either. It will almost certainly result in boring papers (especially boring conclusions). If you have done a good job establishing your points in the body of the paper, the reader already knows and understands your argument. There is no need to merely reiterate. Do not just summarize your main points in your conclusion. Such a boring and mechanical conclusion does nothing to advance your argument or interest your reader. Consider the following conclusion to the paper about gender in *Frankenstein*.

In conclusion, Shelley uses ideas about gender in her novel. Frankenstein and Elizabeth are examples. Shelley offers some interpretations of gender roles through her characterizations. We should all remember that.

Besides starting with a mechanical transitional device, this conclusion does little more than summarize the main points of the outline (and it does not even touch on all of them). It is incomplete and uninteresting.

Instead, your conclusion should add something to your paper. A good tactic is to build upon the points you have been arguing. Asking "why?" often helps you draw further conclusions. For example, in the paper on *Frankenstein*, you might speculate or explain how the concept of gender roles speaks to how Shelley is presenting female characters in the novel in order to convey her beliefs about gender equality. Another method for successfully concluding a paper is to speculate on other directions in which to take your topic by tying it into larger issues. You might do this by envisioning your paper as just one section of a larger paper. Having established your points in this paper, how would you build upon this argument? Where would you go next? In the following conclusion to the paper on *Frankenstein*, the author reiterates some of the main points of the paper but does so in order to amplify the discussion of the novel's treatment of gender and to connect it to arguments about Shelley's intentions:

> By examining the vices and follies of the men in *Frankenstein*, it is demonstrated that, while it may be a male-character-driven novel, the powerful voice of women, and the helm of its authoress, are still highly prevalent. Showing that women are powerful by effects rather than direct reason, Shelley is using intelligence and cleverness to demonstrate that males may not be as superior to females as they may expect.

Citations and Formatting

Using Primary Sources

As the examples included in this chapter indicate, strong papers on literary texts incorporate quotations from the text in order to support their points. It is not enough for you to assert your interpretation without providing support or evidence from the text. Without well-chosen quotations to support your argument, you are, in effect, saying to the reader, "Take my word for it." It is important to use quotations thoughtfully and selectively. Remember that the paper presents *your* argument, so choose quotations that support *your* assertions. Do not let the author's voice overwhelm your own. With that caution in mind, there are some guidelines you should follow to ensure that you use quotations clearly and effectively.

Integrate Quotations

Quotations should always be integrated into your own prose. Do not just drop them into your paper without introduction or comment. Otherwise, it is unlikely that your reader will see their function. You can integrate textual support easily and clearly with identifying tags, short phrases that identify the speaker. For example:

> Frankenstein laments, "the wickedness of my promise burst upon me"

While this tag appears before the quotation, you can also use tags after or in the middle of the quoted text, as the following examples demonstrate:

> "For the first time," clarifies Frankenstein.
>
> "Little happiness remains for us on earth," Frankenstein tells Elizabeth, "yet all that I may one day enjoy is concentered [sic] in you"

You can also use a colon to formally introduce a quotation:

> It is clear that their bond is uncommonly strong: "I love you tenderly . . . remember me with affection"

When you quote brief sections of poems (three lines or fewer), use slash marks to indicate the line breaks in the poem:

> As the poem ends, Dickinson speaks of the power of the imagination: "The revery alone will do, / If bees are few."

Longer quotations (more than four lines of prose or three lines of poetry) should be set off from the rest of your paper in a block quotation. Double-space before you begin the passage, indent it 10 spaces from your left-hand margin, and double-space the passage itself. Because the indentation signals the inclusion of a quotation, do not use quotation marks around the cited passage. Use a colon to introduce the passage:

> Algernon has clear views on marriage at the beginning of the play:

> I really don't see anything romantic in proposing.
> It is very romantic to be in love. But there is
> nothing romantic about a definite proposal. Why,
> one may be accepted. One usually is, I believe.
> Then the excitement is all over. The very essence
> of romance is uncertainty. If ever I get married,
> I'll certainly try to forget the fact.

Clearly, Algernon regards himself as a confirmed bachelor.

The whole of Dickinson's poem speaks of the imagination:

> To make a prairie it takes a clover and one bee,
> One clover, and a bee,
> And revery.
> The revery alone will do,
> If bees are few.

Clearly, she argues for the creative power of the mind.

It is also important to interpret quotations after you introduce them and explain how they help advance your point. You cannot assume that your reader will interpret the quotations the same way that you do.

Quote Accurately

Always quote accurately. Anything within quotations marks must be the author's exact words. There are, however, some rules to follow if you need to modify the quotation to fit into your prose.

1. Use brackets to indicate any material that might have been added to the author's exact wording. For example, if you need to add any words to the quotation or alter it grammatically to allow it to fit into your prose, indicate your changes in brackets:

> Frankenstein confesses to Elizabeth that "if
> [he sees] but one smile on [her] lips," he will
> be content.

2. Conversely, if you choose to omit any words from the quotation, use ellipses (three spaced periods) to indicate missing words or phrases:

> Walton writes to his sister, "I love you tenderly
> . . . remember me with affection"

3. If you delete a sentence or more, use the ellipses after a period:

> Algernon defends himself to Jack: "It isn't. . . .
> It accounts for the extraordinary number of
> bachelors that one sees all over the place"

4. If you omit a line or more of poetry, or more than one paragraph of prose, use a single line of spaced periods to indicate the omission:

> To make a prairie it takes a clover and one bee,
> . . . .
> And revery.
> The revery alone will do,
> If bees are few.

Punctuate Properly

Punctuation of quotations often causes more trouble than it should. Once again, you just need to keep these simple rules in mind.

1. Periods and commas should be placed inside quotation marks, even if they are not part of the original quotation:

> Frankenstein laments, "the wickedness of my
> promise burst upon me."

The only exception to this rule is when the quotation is followed by a parenthetical reference. In this case, the period or comma goes after the citation:

> Frankenstein laments, "the wickedness of my promise burst upon me" (Shelley 114).

2. Other marks of punctuation—colons, semicolons, question marks, and exclamation points—go outside the quotation marks unless they are part of the original quotation:

> Why do some scholars assert that *Frankenstein* "is a text frequently read as a critical portrait of Percy"?

Documenting Primary Sources

Unless you are instructed otherwise, you should provide sufficient information for your reader to locate material you quote. Generally, literature papers follow the rules set forth by the Modern Language Association (MLA). These can be found in the *MLA Handbook for Writers of Research Papers* (seventh edition). You should be able to find this book in the reference section of your library. Additionally, its rules for citing both primary and secondary sources are widely available from reputable online sources. One of these is the Online Writing Lab (OWL) at Purdue University. OWL's guide to MLA style is available at http://owl.english. purdue.edu/owl/resource/557/01/. The Modern Language Association also offers answers to frequently asked questions about MLA style on this helpful Web page: http://www.mla.org/style_faq. Generally, when you are citing from literary works in papers, you should keep a few guidelines in mind.

Parenthetical Citations

MLA asks for parenthetical references in your text after quotations. When you are working with prose (short stories, novels, or essays), include page numbers in the parentheses:

```
Frankenstein  laments,  "the  wickedness  of  my  promise
burst upon me" (Shelley 114).
```

When you are quoting poetry, include line numbers:

```
Dickinson's speaker tells of the arrival of a fly: "There
interposed a Fly- / With Blue-uncertain stumbling Buzz-
/ Between the light-and Me-" (12-14).
```

Works Cited Page

These parenthetical citations are linked to a separate works cited page at the end of the paper. The works cited page lists works alphabetically by the authors' last name. An entry for the above reference to Shelley's *Frankenstein* would read:

```
Shelley, Mary. Frankenstein. 1818. Ed. J. Paul Hunter.
New York: Norton & Company, 1996. Print.
```

The *MLA Handbook* includes a full listing of sample entries, as do many of the online explanations of MLA style.

Documenting Secondary Sources

To ensure that your paper is built entirely upon your own ideas and analysis, instructors often ask that you write interpretative papers without any outside research. If, on the other hand, your paper requires research, you must document any secondary sources you use. You need to document direct quotations, summaries or paraphrases of others' ideas, and factual information that is not common knowledge. Follow the guidelines above for quoting primary sources when you use direct quotations from secondary sources. Keep in mind that MLA style also includes specific guidelines for citing electronic sources. OWL's Web site provides a good summary: http://owl.english.purdue.edu/owl/resource/557/09/.

Parenthetical Citations

As with the documentation of primary sources, described above, MLA guidelines require in-text parenthetical references to your secondary sources. Unlike the research papers you might write for a history class, literary research papers following MLA style do not use footnotes as a means of documenting sources. Instead, after a quotation, you should cite the author's last name and the page number:

> Frankenstein laments, "the wickedness of my promise burst upon me" (Shelley 114).

If you include the name of the author in your prose, then you would include only the page number in your citation. For example:

> Shelley makes it clear that Frankenstein laments, "the wickedness of my promise burst upon me" (114).

If you are including more than one work by the same author, the parenthetical citation should include a shortened yet identifiable version of the title in order to indicate which of the author's works you cite. For example:

> As Mary Poovey suggests, Shelley felt a pressure to produce "imaginative" writings as a way of "proving her worth" ("My Hideous Progeny" 115).

Similarly, and just as important, if you summarize or paraphrase the particular ideas of your source, you must provide documentation:

> Frankenstein often expresses great regret and sadness (Shelley 114).

Works Cited Page
Like the primary sources discussed above, the parenthetical references to secondary sources are keyed to a separate works cited page at the end of your paper. Here is an example of a works cited page that uses the examples cited above. Note that when two or more works by the same author are listed, you should use three hyphens followed by a period in the subsequent entries. You can find a complete list of sample entries in the *MLA Handbook* or from a reputable online summary of MLA style.

Works Cited Page

London, Bette. "Mary Shelley, *Frankenstein*, and the Spectacle of Masculinity." *PMLA* 108.2 (1993): 253-67. Print.

Poovey, Mary. "My Hideous Progeny: Mary Shelley and the Feminization of Romanticism." *PMLA* 95.3 (1980): 332-47. Print.

Shelley, Mary. *Frankenstein*. 1818. Ed. J. Paul Hunter. New York: Norton & Company, 1996. Print.

Wohlpart, A. James. "A Tradition of Male Poetics: Mary Shelley's *Frankenstein* as an Allegory of Art." *Midwest Quarterly: A Journal of Contemporary Thought* 39.3 (1998): 265-79. Print.

Plagiarism

Failure to document carefully and thoroughly can leave you open to charges of stealing the ideas of others, which is known as plagiarism, and this is a very serious matter. Remember that it is important to include quotation marks when you use language from your source, even if you use just one or two words. For example, if you wrote, Frankenstein laments the wickedness of his promise, you would be guilty of plagiarism, since you used Shelley's distinct language without acknowledging her as the source. Instead, you should write: Frankenstein laments, "the wickedness of my promise burst upon me" (Shelley 114). In this case, you have properly credited Shelley.

Similarly, neither summarizing the ideas of an author nor changing or omitting just a few words means that you can omit a citation. Vyvyan Holland's book, *Son of Oscar Wilde*, contains the following passage:

Most small boys adore their fathers, and we adored ours; and as all good fathers are, he was a hero to us both. . . . There was nothing about him of the monster that some people who never knew him and never even saw him have tried to make him out to be. He was a real companion to us, and we always looked forward eagerly to his frequent visits to our nursery. Most parents in those days were far too solemn and pompous with

their children, insisting on a vast amount of usually
undeserved respect. My own father was quite different;
he had so much of the child in his own nature that he
delighted in playing our games (Holland 52).

Below are two examples of plagiarized passages:

Vyvyan Holland loved his father, and like a lot of kids,
really looked up to him. He did not know the vicious
person that many people believed Wilde to be. All he
knew was that his father was not serious and overly
inflated like many parents.

Holland contends that his father was quite different,
especially given the fact that he was very much a child
in his own nature (Holland 52).

While the first passage does not use Holland's exact language, it does list
some of the same examples as the book. Since this interpretation is Holland's distinct idea, this constitutes plagiarism. The second passage has
shortened his passage, changed some wording, and included a citation,
but some of the phrasing is Holland's. The first passage could be fixed
with a parenthetical citation. Because some of the wording in the second
remains the same, though, it would require the use of quotation marks,
in addition to a parenthetical citation. The passage below represents an
honestly and adequately documented use of the original passage:

Vyvyan Holland remembers his childhood very fondly:
"Most small boys adore their fathers, and we adored
ours; and as all good fathers are, he was a hero to us
both. . . . There nothing about him of the monster
that some people who never knew him and never even saw
him have tried to make him out to be" (52).

This passage acknowledges that the interpretation is derived from
Holland while appropriately using quotations to indicate his precise
language.

While it is not necessary to document well-known facts, often referred to as "common knowledge," any ideas or language that you take from someone else must be properly documented. Common knowledge generally includes the birth and death dates of authors or other well-documented facts of their lives. An often-cited guideline is that if you can find the information in three sources, it is common knowledge. Despite this guideline, it is, admittedly, often difficult to know if the facts you uncover are common knowledge or not. When in doubt, document your source.

Sample Essay

Kelsey Raasch
Dr. Steinwand
ENG 336
April 12, 2010

THE FEMALE IN *FRANKENSTEIN*

If asked to find a novel that clearly illustrated the superiority of the male sex, some might naïvely point to Mary Shelley's *Frankenstein*. Upfront we see a tale dominated by male characters; in fact, the few females who are present embody rather vacant personas, serving as functions rather than as people. However, when one considers the role of females in the grand scheme of the novel, we are able to understand the importance of the female in the work as well as in the theme that Shelley is conveying. While it can be said that the males in *Frankenstein* embody female voices through the inherent fact that they are written by a woman, through their very masculine flaws and actions, the male characters support and uphold the importance of the female role in society. By insisting that the woman only serves as a function, that function becomes more relevant as the male figures try to phase females out of the story altogether. Thus *Frankenstein* becomes a cautionary tale of what happens when men try to live without women, and clearly it has disastrous results.

There are two distinct lenses with which to examine the males' ignorance toward women in the novel, as well as its extenuating implications. The first is the demanding of a woman as a complementary partner, and the second is the usurpation of the female's role in reproduction.

The three distinct male characters that the readers are introduced to at the beginning of the novel are Walton, Frankenstein, and for all intents and purposes the creature—or at least the idea of the masculine creature is introduced. All of these males have some sort of female partner or are in search of a female partner. Mary Poovey describes this need as the male characters wanting to reach maturity: "[Shelley] continues to dramatize personal fulfillment . . . with the absent mother being replaced by the closest female equivalent . . . the beloved object would be sought and found only within the comforting confines of preexistent domestic relationships" (Poovey 335). With this in mind then, it seems that the men need to fully fulfill themselves by finding a companion, but not just any companion—one that domestically would help heal them from the pain of an absent mother. Through this, the males choose women who are familial but, as literary characters, appear only to serve as a function. Walton has found his "more than sister" in Mrs. Saville and addresses and signs the letters in a way that suggests that their bond is uncommonly strong: "I love you tenderly . . . remember me with affection" (Shelley 12). He uses his sister as a vessel to tell the story and uses her as a springboard to give him comfort, though not once are we given any inclination as to the character of Mrs. Saville herself. She remains an empty canvas, a theme that can also be conveyed in Victor's "more than sister," Elizabeth Larenza.

Elizabeth is declared to be Victor's mate, and Victor acknowledges this without actually knowing how

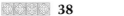

she feels about the match. It was his mother's dying wish, and rather than pursue the courting facet of the relationship, both characters assume the wish as fact. Toward the end of the novel, in a letter that Elizabeth writes to Victor, we are presented with her feelings, "if I see but one smile on your lips when we meet . . . I shall need no other happiness" (Shelley 130), but these sentiments seem to come rather unsupported. We understand through this letter that Elizabeth loves Victor, but the events or feelings that led to this are absent, furthering the argument that Elizabeth's role in the novel is as a literary function, not a character. All that is important is that Elizabeth is meant for Victor, and Victor depends on Elizabeth for his happiness, especially after his multiple confrontations with the creature: "'[L]ittle happiness remains for us on earth; yet all that I may one day enjoy is concentered [sic] in you," (Shelley 131). The creature, also, does not want to be deprived of a female companion. After seeing Felix's and Safie's relationship, Adam and Eve's in *Paradise Lost*, as well as Victor's and Elizabeth's, the creature only finds it fitting that he gain a female companion of his own. Since the female is never fully created, she is the least developed of the other female "leads." Their purpose is shown to be a simple companion, a function in which the woman serves as a vessel of completeness and not as an actual human character. Several scholars have commented that Mary Shelley in certain aspects of her life is considered to be the completion and companion of her husband, Percy Shelley. One such scholar is Bette London, who states that *Frankenstein*, "Mary Shelley's most famous creation," is "a text frequently read as a critical portrait of Percy" (London 255). This interpretation of *Frankenstein* then suggests an autobiographical tone. Mary's purpose was to serve as companion to Percy Shelley, though, as her strong mother, Mary Wollstonecraft, asserted, women should be able to stand alone.

Returning back to the females we are presented with, all are underdeveloped characters meant to serve as stand-ins for other ideas or purposes. However, it is insinuated with all three that if they were asked to help their respective mates and show their personalities, their male counterparts would not meet with their tragic ends, and woman would have effectively saved the man. Walton's sister could have perhaps shown or written Walton the errors and problems that could result from his venture and would have spared him the loneliness that he experienced throughout his journey. More significantly are the impacts that it could have had for Victor and his creation. Victor was presented with the opportunity to tell Elizabeth what was happening, but Victor rejected the idea of talking to her, instead relying on his masculine instincts to take care of the problem. Shelley creates doubt that this was always the plan, that it would have always ended in the same situation by keeping Elizabeth's personality a mystery. There is no specific marker to show that Elizabeth could have prevented the final outcome, but as we know little about her, there is no way of being certain. Likewise, we know nothing about the creature's female, but she more than any other female could have altered the events of the novel. If all the monster needed was a female, then the creation of her could have been the solution to his loneliness and need for revenge, effectively resolving the conflict of the novel.

Though it is not insinuated that the males are trying to phase out the females from their world, especially given the previous argument that they need women, Frankenstein's purpose of creating an ideal male, without a female involved, changes the perception of how reproduction is supposed to occur and leads us to the argument of the usurpation of the female in reproduction.

James Wohlpart argues that Shelley writes in a time when literature was dominated by males, and as such, most of the creation, so to speak, fell within the hands of the males and bypassed the females: "[Shelly] also implicates the tradition which led up to this period, suggesting that artistic creativity has predominately become . . . a male pursuit" (Wohlpart 266). Thus Shelley takes back the role of the female in art and demonstrates that one cannot have art and beauty without a woman. In short, nothing can be produced without a woman being involved in some way. Thus when Frankenstein attempts to do just that, the disastrous results that occur prove all the wrong that has been unleashed by trying to create life with only male entities.

Compounding this idea is the concept of the two creatures of both sexes procreating. While Frankenstein found it, at least on some basic level, ethical, he cannot create a woman. He is concerned that the creation of a female monster will allow the two to procreate and produce a plague of little monsters; "the first results of those sympathies for which the demon thirsted would be children, and a race of devils would be propagated upon the earth, who might make the very existence of the species of man a condition precarious of being deserted by one of his own species" (Shelley 114). It is at this point that Frankenstein comes to understand the implications and the loss of morality that creating against nature's will has on the cycle of life; as a result, for the first time, "the wickedness of my promise burst upon me" (Shelley 114). Already people have died, and Frankenstein, at this point, comes to understand the ethical concerns of creating life unnaturally. To create without both sexes is against the rules of nature. He then destroys the female that he had begun working on and comes to the conclusion that men are not made to solely hold life in their hands. This idea, coupled with the fact that women are consistently pushed to the edges of the narrative, reveals that ignoring the power and influence of women only results in miscalculation. Shelley thus proves by bad example why men need women in society, as much as they may wish otherwise.

By examining the vices and follies of the men in *Frankenstein*, it is demonstrated that, while it may be a male-character-driven novel, the powerful voice of women, and the helm of its authoress, are still highly prevalent. Showing that women are powerful by effects rather than direct reason, Shelley is using intelligence and cleverness to demonstrate that males may not be as superior to females as they may expect.

WORKS CITED

London, Bette. "Mary Shelley, *Frankenstein*, and the Spectacle of Masculinity." *PMLA* 108.2 (1993): 253–67. Print.

Poovey, Mary. "My Hideous Progeny: Mary Shelley and the Feminization of Romanticism." *PMLA* 95.3 (1980): 332–47. Print.

Shelley, Mary. *Frankenstein*. 1818. Ed. J. Paul Hunter. New York: Norton & Company, 1996. Print.

Wohlpart, A. James. "A Tradition of Male Poetics: Mary Shelley's *Frankenstein* as an Allegory of Art." *Midwest Quarterly: A Journal of Contemporary Thought* 39.3 (1998): 265–79. Print.

HOW TO WRITE ABOUT MARY SHELLEY

HER LEGACY

MARY WOLLSTONECRAFT Shelley wrote a number of novels, stories, and journals, some of which have only recently been rediscovered. Yet she is remembered almost exclusively for *Frankenstein*, a novel that she began writing at eighteen years old, a work that has impacted the literary world and the cultural and popular consciousness deeply. Scholar Anne K. Mellor writes, "*Frankenstein* is our culture's most penetrating literary analysis of the psychology of modern 'scientific' man, of the dangers inherent in scientific research, and of the horrifying but predictable consequences of an uncontrolled technological exploitation of nature and the female" ("Making" 9). It seems that Shelley left us a legacy of questions that we perhaps have yet to properly answer.

Literary scholars and historians wonder how a young woman of eighteen became emboldened and imaginative enough to create such a dark and original tale, yet biographers say that Shelley "was as remarkable for her self-possession as for her keen, intelligent mind. Only someone who knew her well could guess at the dark imagination operating behind her serene smile and large-eyed gaze" (Seymour 150). At the time that she began *Frankenstein,* she had already lost one baby and was deep into her relationship with Percy Bysshe Shelley, who was still married. Yet Shelley had no idea of the troubles that would ensnare her before long.

Only 500 copies of the first edition of *Frankenstein* were printed, and it was not immediately reprinted once those copies sold out. Shelley's significantly revised edition appeared in 1831, yet in 1823, the play *Presumption, or the Fate of Frankenstein* by Richard Brinsley Peake was staged in London. Peake created the "goofball servant . . . bumbling assistant . . . hunchback" character, while also in his play, Frankenstein calls out the now famous line, "It lives! It lives!" and the creature does not speak, all elements that are staples of the tale as we know it now (Hitchcock 83). "By the end of 1823 five different retellings of *Frankenstein*" premiered in London (Hitchcock 88).

Retellings of *Frankenstein* all seem to contain the same elements that are not in Shelley's tale: "an inarticulate monster, a bumbling laboratory assistant, an angry crowd in search of the monster, and a cataclysmic ending in which creature and creator perish together. The public eagerly grasped this monster of a story, told and retold it, reshaping it as they did" (Hitchcock 88). This is why the novel is still so compelling. Not because we already know the story, although most of us think we do, but precisely because we do not know the story, and Shelley surprises and fascinates us with themes, characters, suspense, and frights that endure.

Frankenstein was published anonymously at first, a common practice at the time. Ironically, it seems that by the time Shelley was identified as the author of the novel and a version of the story had achieved a degree of popularity, Shelley's own interest had waned:

> when, in later life, [Shelley] spoke of creature and book in one breath as 'my hideous progeny' and invited it to 'go forth and prosper', she was aware that dramatized versions had already drained its life-fluid while hugely increasing its fame. *Frankenstein,* as performed on stage, became a spooky comic melodrama while the Creature, seized on by political cartoonists, became a symbol of danger, subversiveness and menace. By 1831, when she wished her new edition commercial prosperity, her serious intentions had, like the Creature in the novel's closing words, been 'borne away . . . lost in darkness and distance' (Seymour 173).

Contemporary reviews wavered between disgust and fascination, calling the novel "audacious and impious" but also "praising the author's inventive talent and descriptive gifts" (Seymour 196). One reviewer laments that the novel "leav[es] the wearied reader, after a struggle between laughter and loathing, in doubt whether the head or the heart of the author be the most diseased" (Croker 385). At the same time, another reviewer gushes: "Frankenstein is, I think, the best instance of natural passions applied to supernatural events that I ever met with" (Anonymous *Knight's* 196).

In 1819, the year after *Frankenstein* was published, a pamphleteer wrote of Byron and his "Vampyre crew," noting that one of the "fresh monsters" the group (Polidori, Shelley, Byron) had created was "'the wretch abhorred' by the name of Frankenstein." This is the first known instance of the creature being called by its creator's name, a habit that quickly caught on and never waned (Hitchcock 79).

Frankenstein has been translated into many genres and forms, most of them famous in their own day as well as now. Boris Karloff plays the creature in the 1931 *Frankenstein,* the 1935 *Bride of Frankenstein,* and the 1939 *Son of Frankenstein.* It is well known that Karloff had a soft spot for the creature, although he also played Victor Frankenstein in *Frankenstein 1970,* released in 1958. The first film adaptation of *Frankenstein* was Edison Studio's 1910 *Frankenstein.* Two decades after that saw the 1932 radio broadcast, and a host of adaptations followed, including Disney's *Frankenweenie, The Munsters* television show, *The Rocky Horror Picture Show,* and Mel Brooks's *Young Frankenstein.* There are also movies about Shelley and the conception of *Frankenstein,* including *Haunted Summer, Rowing with the Wind,* and *Gothic.* Continuations and retellings persist in print, too, with books such as Theodore Roszak's *The Memoirs of Elizabeth Frankenstein,* Peter Ackroyd's *The Casebook of Victor Frankenstein,* and Dean Koontz's *Frankenstein* trilogy.

HER INFLUENCES

Mary Shelley's influences seem a bit heady to us now, given her literary parentage and the legendary circle of friends she kept as an adult. Clearly her strongest influences were her parents, feminist philosopher Mary Wollstonecraft, who died a few days after Mary was born, and William Godwin, revered novelist and intellectual.

In her adult life, Shelley met, ran away with, and eventually married Percy Bysshe Shelley, whose writing she worked to publish after he died in 1822. Shelley was friends with John Polidori, Lord Byron, Leigh Hunt, and Washington Irving, among others.

Mary Shelley was not afraid to disagree with friends and family, positing views in her work that countered those of her husband and father. Her contemporary audience often missed the political commentary in her works, and only recently has she been recognized as an author and thinker in her own right, rather than a footnote to her father's or husband's lives.

It seems that Shelley's own life was perhaps her greatest influence. Her firstborn child, a girl, was born 18 months before the idea for *Frankenstein* came about. The baby died at two weeks old, and Shelley had a recurring dream that she recorded in her journal: "Dream that my little baby came to life again—that it had only been cold & that we rubbed it by the fire & it lived—I awake & find no baby" (Shelley *Journals* 70). It is not far-fetched to imagine a wish to create life or, more importantly, to reanimate a once-living creature, arising from this heartbreaking instance.

HER WORK

Mary Shelley's work as a whole shows some of the influences of her professional and personal life. A familiarity with her life, however, is not necessary for doing intriguing analysis of Shelley's work. This volume will guide you through general approaches to her fiction. The remainder of this section will discuss some of the notable elements of Shelley's work: the patterns in her use of themes; her construction of character; the history and context of her writing; the philosophy underlying her book; and her use of symbolism, imagery, and language.

Themes

There is a range of themes in *Frankenstein* just waiting to be addressed in scholarly detail. Perhaps one of the most commonly discussed themes of the novel is "Victor Frankenstein's total failure as a parent" (Mellor "Making" 10). Mary Wollstonecraft writes, "great proportion of the misery that wanders, in hideous forms, around the world, is allowed to rise from the negligence of parents" (Wollstonecraft 246). Scholars often wonder what role Shelley's gender plays in this parenting theme in addition to considering the role her own life played. Her mother died only a few days after Shelley was born, and as a teenager Shelley was rejected, then shunned by her father after running off with Percy Shelley. Shelley biographer Miranda Seymour writes that "*Frankenstein* can easily be turned into a biographer's sandpit, but Mary's story of promethean ambition, of rejection, the denial of love, and the danger of judging by appearances, was intended to carry the weight of a social message. What may have begun as an extension of the story of an Arctic explorer, or as a gothic tale for fireside thrills, was developed as a vehicle for ideas and social criticism" (Seymour 173).

Characters

Shelley's characters may be the most unusual elements of the novel. A number of characters, in addition to the creature, are real and yet supernatural, endearing and infuriating, deeply flawed and frustratingly, unrealistically perfect. We can pose many questions about the novel and Shelley's possible intentions. She perhaps modeled characters after people in her own life, as she was known to do in other works. Maybe all of her characters fluctuate between best- and worst-case scenarios, and their unsteady senses of themselves lead them to fluctuate between good and evil actions. Perhaps all of her characters live in a morally nebulous in-between space, where simplistic distinctions cannot be easily made between good and evil, right and wrong, or black and white.

History and Context

The dramatic story of how Shelley first dreamed elements of the story of *Frankenstein*, and then longed to terrify her readers as she had been frightened by the dream, is fascinating, legendary, and possibly exaggerated. John Polidori, the only one of the group in Geneva who kept a journal at the time (or whose journal still exists), seems to contradict Shelley's dramatic story, yet the story's effect is still felt (Seymour 157).

The aspects of horror that are woven into *Frankenstein* stem from the creature's haunting words and aspect, from Frankenstein's reaction to the creature, and from both characters' ruminations on the world and humanity as a whole. Shelley was well informed about current events and does not hesitate to place current ideologies as well as criticisms of the same into the novel. An anonymous contemporary reviewer writes, "There never was a wilder story imagined, yet, like most of the fictions

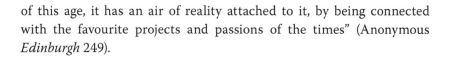

of this age, it has an air of reality attached to it, by being connected with the favourite projects and passions of the times" (Anonymous *Edinburgh* 249).

Philosophy and Ideas

As the daughter of two outspoken and well-respected writers, thinkers, and philosophers, it is not a stretch to imagine Mary Shelley holding a wealth of sharply defined views on any number of topics. *Frankenstein* alone is packed with views on religion, knowledge, and how the two are acquired, used, and, most importantly, misused. Percy Bysshe Shelley's review of *Frankenstein* claims that the novel's moral is "Treat a person ill, and he will become wicked" (Robinson 435). Is it that simple, though? Considering the radical ideological shifts that occurred just before Shelley's birth (the French Revolution) as well as during her lifetime (romanticism, the Industrial Revolution), it is easy to see how her philosophies and ideas could be numerous and ever changing.

Form and Genre

According to Mary Shelley's introduction to the 1831 edition, we have Percy Bysshe Shelley to thank for the fact that *Frankenstein* became a full-length novel: "At first I thought but of a few pages—of a short tale; but Shelley urged me to develope [sic] the idea at greater length. I certainly did not owe the suggestion of one incident, nor scarcely of one train of feeling, to my husband, and yet but for his incitement, it would never have taken the form in which it was presented to the world" (Robinson 442). While the length and complexity of the novel are partially attributable to the author's husband, it is less clear what influences supplied Shelley with the elements of science fiction with which she imbued her tale and heralded a new literary genre.

Shelley's status as a woman, not to mention a busy (and often grieving) wife and mother, make her stereotypically unlikely to become the first science fiction writer. The author's adage states, "Write what you know," and we wonder to what degree Shelley did this. This belief that the novel's themes were primarily motivated by autobiographical concerns has been taken up by many scholars who frequently link key elements of the book to Shelley's own parenting issues and grief over lost children. It helps us to understand how Shelley could have conceived these ideas in the first place. We will probably never know exactly how or why Shelley developed her ideas and launched a new genre, but we can see clearly that the work that resulted has stood the test of time.

Language, Symbols, and Imagery

You wake slowly to find a creature, larger than life, hideously ugly, part man, part beast, standing over you, staring with watery, yellow eyes. Does imagery get any more vividly immediate or potentially frightening than that? The irony of *Frankenstein* is that the imagery, symbolism, and language in the novel are vivid, fresh, and infused with elements of the fantastic and yet many of these central elements are altered in adaptations or retellings. These changes could be the result of other writers and screenwriters feeling they cannot improve on Shelley's work or capture its subtleties and complexities, so they simplify Shelley's approach and treatment, often fixating on the monstrous and macabre elements of the tale.

Another compelling aspect of the imagery in the novel is that it is accessible, clear and easy for readers to picture throughout. The suggestion of terror is more vivid than the actual acts of terror that drive the plot forward. We are told about the horrifying instances but never actually shown them. Perhaps Shelley's true genius in regard to imagery was in allowing the readers' imaginations to take over.

FINAL WORDS

While *Frankenstein,* in its original form, as Shelley conceived of and presented it, may give many of us nightmares, it eventually became a balm for Shelley herself. In the introduction to the 1831 edition, Shelley writes of the way the book soothes her: "And now, once again, I bid my hideous progeny go forth and prosper. I have an affection for it, for it was the offspring of happy days, when death and grief were but words, which found no true echo in my heart. Its several pages speak of many a walk, many a drive, and many a conversation, when I was not alone; and my companion was one whom, in this world, I shall never see more" (Robinson 442).

Bibliography for How to Write about Mary Shelley

Anonymous. From *Knight's Quarterly.* 3 (August–November 1824): 195–99. Print.

Croker, John. From the *Quarterly Review.* 36 (January 1818): 379–85. Print.

Forry, Steven Earl. *Hideous Progenies: Dramatizations of Frankenstein from Mary Shelley to the Present.* Philadelphia: U of Pennsylvania P, 1990. Print.

Fraistat, Neil and Steven E. Jones, eds. "Mary Wollstonecraft Shelley." *Romantic Circles.* 28 June 1999. Web. 26 May 2010.

Hitchcock, Susan Tyler. *Frankenstein: A Cultural History.* New York: W.W. Norton, 2007. Print.

Holmes, Richard. *The Age of Wonder: How the Romantic Generation Discovered the Beauty and Terror of Science.* New York: Vintage, 2008. Print.

Hoobler, Dorothy and Thomas Hoobler. *The Monsters: Mary Shelley and the Curse of Frankenstein.* New York: Little, Brown, 2006. Print.

The Journals of Mary Shelley, 1814–44. Paula R. Feldman and Diana Scott-Kilvert, eds. 2 vols. Oxford: Oxford UP, 1987. Print.

Mellor, Anne K. "Making a 'Monster': An Introduction to *Frankenstein.*" *The Cambridge Companion to Mary Shelley.* Ed. Esther Schor. Cambridge: Cambridge UP, 2003. 9–25. Print.

———. *Mary Shelley: Her Life, Her Fiction, Her Monsters.* New York: Methuen, 1988. Print.

Moers, Ellen. *Literary Women.* Garden City, N.Y.: Doubleday, 1976. Print.

Morton, Timothy, ed. *Mary Shelley's Frankenstein: A Sourcebook.* London: Routledge, 2002. Print.

Pridmore, Jan. "Mary Shelley." *Literary History.* 17 April 2010. Web. 26 May 2010.

Robinson, Charles E., ed. *The Original Frankenstein: Mary Shelley's Earliest Draft and Percy Shelley's Revised Text.* 1816–1817. By Mary Wollstonecraft Shelley with Percy Bysshe Shelley. New York: Vintage, 2008. Print.

Schor, Esther, ed. *The Cambridge Companion to Mary Shelley.* Cambridge: Cambridge UP, 2003. Print.

Seymour, Miranda. *Mary Shelley.* New York: Grove Press, 2000. Print.

Shelley, Mary Wollstonecraft with Percy Bysshe Shelley. *Frankenstein; or, The Modern Prometheus.* The Original Two-Volume Novel of 1816–1817 from the Bodleian Library Manuscripts. Ed. Charles E. Robinson. New York: Vintage Books, 2008. Print.

Voller, Jack G. "Mary Shelley." *The Literary Gothic.* 27 April 2010. Web. 26 May 2010.

Wollstonecraft, Mary. *A Vindication of the Rights of Woman.* 1792. Ed. Sylvana Tomaselli. Cambridge: Cambridge UP, 1995. Print.

THE HISTORY OF
FRANKENSTEIN

FRANKENSTEIN IS one of relatively few novels that have transcended classic status to become a phenomenon. What is it about this book that has stood the test of time? Perhaps a more nuanced question would be, how has *Frankenstein* both succeeded and failed at standing the test of time? Do adaptations in film and print enhance or take away from the original novel? What would Shelley think about what her work has become and has come to mean today? Why is it that some novels become a part of culture and history in ways that most cannot?

One interpretation of *Frankenstein*'s status addresses the wealth of ideas that readers can gain from an encounter with the novel:

> *Frankenstein* is a great work because we can read what we will from it. It has the resilience, the elasticity and the power of a myth. Writers and critics have, since Mary's death, uncovered more ways of interpreting it than the young author can ever have dreamed of. . . . She, like her creature, was unfairly condemned, judged not for what she was, but for how appearances made her seem. The fact that she was not married to Shelley did not make her wicked, any more than the Creature's unnatural birth and bizarre appearance made him evil (Seymour 172).

Strategies

This section of the chapter addresses various topic suggestions for writing about the history of *Frankenstein*. Also broached are general methods for approaching these topics. These writing prompts are in no way exhaustive and are meant to provide a jumping-off point rather than an answer key or a blueprint to the perfect essay. Use these suggestions to find your own ideas and form your own analyses. All topics discussed in this chapter could turn into strong, original essays.

Sample Topics:

1. **The literary canon:** Does *Frankenstein* belong in the literary canon?

The literary canon is the collection of literature considered influential in shaping culture. There is a bit of a cyclical relationship between the creation of the canon and the literature most often taught in schools. Is the literature taught in schools because it is in the canon, or is the literature in the canon because it is most often taught in schools? How frequently is *Frankenstein* taught in schools? Why? Mary Shelley is not often considered part of the romantic circle, generally understood to include William Wordsworth, Samuel Taylor Coleridge, John Keats, William Blake, Percy Bysshe Shelley, and George Gordon, Lord Byron. Is she not included, not canonized with this group because she is a woman? Is it because these men primarily wrote poetry while Shelley wrote prose? Is *Frankenstein* simply too different, too far afield from "typical" romantic writing, or typical writing of any kind, to be included? Today, the literary canon often excludes writing that belongs to a particular genre such as mystery, horror, or romance. Is this the case here, too, that because *Frankenstein* is a precursor to the genre of science fiction, it is excluded? Is *Frankenstein* too popular to be included in the canon? What does it mean to be too popular?

2. **Confusion about names:** Why has the creature become known as Frankenstein?

Reviewers, critics, and readers began calling the creature Frankenstein shortly after the novel was published, so Shelley presumably knew about the confusion. Did she ever address this equating the creator with his creation? Does it seem to have bothered her? Is there any chance that she actually wanted readers to confuse the creature with Frankenstein? Did she try to make them so similar as to become interchangeable? Why has the confusion persisted?

3. **Critical reception:** What are twenty-first-century readers' views of the novel?

Critics and reviewers of Shelley's time felt that the novel lacked a clear moral message, posited antireligious views, and drew on gruesome and shocking imagery, all of which should, in their view, repel readers. The book's enduring popularity says otherwise. Are today's readers drawn to the work precisely because of these "negative" reviews? Do we crave societal criticism today in a way that was much less acceptable in Shelley's time? Are we unsatisfied or impatient with Shelley's novel and therefore drawn to film versions or adaptations instead?

4. **Film lore:** Why are almost all of the film versions so vastly different from the novel?

The first stage versions of *Frankenstein*, several of which appeared in Shelley's lifetime, and even before the 1831 revised edition of the novel came out, contained a number of changes to the novel that endure in film versions today: "an inarticulate monster, a bumbling laboratory assistant, an angry crowd in search of the monster, and a cataclysmic ending in which creature and creator perish together" (Hitchcock 88). Why do these changes endure? How has *Frankenstein* become a cult film classic and entered Halloween-related lore? Some of the film versions, most notably Mel Brooks's *Young Frankenstein*, are comedies. Is there anything funny in the original novel? Does Shelley intend to be funny? Why or why not?

Bibliography for the History of *Frankenstein*

Forry, Steven Earl. *Hideous Progenies: Dramatizations of Frankenstein from Mary Shelley to the Present.* Philadelphia: U of Pennsylvania P, 1990. Print.

Fraistat, Neil and Steven E. Jones, eds. "Mary Wollstonecraft Shelley." *Romantic Circles*. 28 June 1999. Web. 26 May 2010.

Hitchcock, Susan Tyler. *Frankenstein: A Cultural History*. New York: W.W. Norton, 2007. Print.

Holmes, Richard. *The Age of Wonder: How the Romantic Generation Discovered the Beauty and Terror of Science*. New York: Vintage, 2008. Print.

Hoobler, Dorothy and Thomas Hoobler. *The Monsters: Mary Shelley and the Curse of Frankenstein*. New York: Little, Brown, 2006. Print.

The Journals of Mary Shelley, 1814–44. Paula R. Feldman and Diana Scott-Kilvert, eds. 2 vols. Oxford: Oxford UP, 1987. Print.

"Mary Wollstonecraft Shelley." *The Literature Network*. n.d. Web. 13 August 2010.

Mellor, Anne K. "Making a 'Monster': An Introduction to *Frankenstein*." *The Cambridge Companion to Mary Shelley*. Ed. Esther Schor. Cambridge: Cambridge UP, 2003. 9–25. Print.

———. *Mary Shelley: Her Life, Her Fiction, Her Monsters*. New York: Methuen, 1988. Print.

Moers, Ellen. *Literary Women*. Garden City, N.Y.: Doubleday, 1976. Print.

Morton, Timothy, ed. *Mary Shelley's Frankenstein: A Sourcebook*. London: Routledge, 2002. Print.

Pridmore, Jan. "Mary Shelley." *Literary History*. 17 April 2010. Web. 26 May 2010.

Robinson, Charles E., ed. *The Original Frankenstein: Mary Shelley's Earliest Draft and Percy Shelley's Revised Text*. 1816–1817. By Mary Wollstonecraft Shelley with Percy Bysshe Shelley. New York: Vintage, 2008. Print.

Schor, Esther, ed. *The Cambridge Companion to Mary Shelley*. Cambridge: Cambridge UP, 2003. Print.

Seymour, Miranda. *Mary Shelley*. New York: Grove Press, 2000. Print.

Shelley, Mary Wollstonecraft with Percy Bysshe Shelley. *Frankenstein; or, The Modern Prometheus*. The Original Two-Volume Novel of 1816–1817 from the Bodleian Library Manuscripts. Ed. Charles E. Robinson. New York: Vintage Books, 2008. Print.

Teuber, Andreas. "Mary Wollstonecraft Shelley." Brandeis University. n.d. Web. 13 August 2010.

Voller, Jack G. "Mary Shelley." *The Literary Gothic*. 27 April 2010. Web. 26 May 2010.

Woodbridge, Kim. "Mary Shelley and *Frankenstein*." 2010. Web. 13 August 2010.

THEMES IN *FRANKENSTEIN*

READING TO WRITE

AFTER WILLIAM, Justine, Henry, Elizabeth, and Frankenstein's father have all died, Frankenstein relates:

What then became of me? I know not. I lost sensation, and chains and darkness were the only objects that pressed upon me. Sometimes, indeed, I dreamed that I wandered in flowery meadows and pleasant vales with the friends of my youth; but I awoke and found myself in a dungeon. Melancholy followed, but by degrees I regained a clear conception of my miseries and situation, and was then released from my prison. For they had called me mad; and during many months, as I understood, a solitary cell had been my habitation. But liberty had been a useless gift to me had I not, as I awakened to reason, at the same time awakened to vengeance. As the memory of past misfortunes pressed upon me, I began to reflect on their cause—the monster whom I had created, the miserable dæmon whom I had sent abroad in the world for my destruction. I was possessed by a maddening rage when I thought of him—and desired and ardently prayed that I might have him within my grasp to wreak a great and signal revenge on his cursed head.

Nor did my hate long confine itself to useless wishes; I began to reflect on the best means of securing him; and for this purpose, about a month after my release, I repaired to a criminal judge in the town and told him that I had an accusation to make, that I knew the destroyer of my family,

55

and that I required him to exert his while authority for the apprehension of the murderer. (Shelley 221)

What does he mean when he says he does not know what became of him? Does he actually not know, or is he unable to articulate or clearly think about it? Is he still that confused? Why or why not? How can you tell? Here, as in many parts of the book, he relates his feelings to nature—"flowery meadows and pleasant vales." Are the dungeon and solitary cell literal? Do they occur only in his mind, in contrast to the beauties and freedoms of nature, or was he actually in a prison-type environment for a while? Who are the "they" that he claims said he was insane? Was he ever actually insane? If he was, has he now recovered his sanity? Is he the best judge of his own capabilities and mental state? How far can we trust him to convey his own story? What does Shelley seem to want readers to believe and understand about Frankenstein's mental state? Why? How can you tell?

Shelley (and/or Frankenstein) never lets us completely separate the creature from Frankenstein. We do not think of the creature without being reminded that it was Frankenstein who created it and then did nothing to help it or stop its violence. Is the vengeance of which Frankenstein speaks a good thing? It is keeping him alive, evidently, and giving him purpose. Are readers expected to admire him for this new mission? Why or why not? How can you tell? Should Frankenstein have become this angry much earlier in the book? What would have happened if he had resolved upon revenge immediately after William was killed? Why does Frankenstein decide that now is a good time to go to the authorities? Why is he no longer afraid of being called insane? How is the magistrate's reaction ironic, given Frankenstein's refusal to involve authorities earlier in the book?

STRATEGIES

This section of the chapter addresses various possible topics for writing about themes in *Frankenstein* as well as general methods for approaching these topics. These suggestions are just a starting point to set you on the path to your own well-developed discussion of the novel. The themes in *Frankenstein* proliferate. Use these suggestions to find your own ideas and form your own analyses.

Themes

Readers can find any number of themes in a novel, especially one as widely read as *Frankenstein*. A theme can be defined as an idea or concept that helps to inform the plot; it is often found by looking carefully at words, phrases, and chapter titles in the novel. When more than one character undergoes the same or similar experiences or when there is notable repetition of an action or idea, you have unearthed and identified a theme. The next step is to ask what the book is saying about the theme and how and if that commentary changes. Do characters have differing opinions on the given theme? Does the author seem to want readers to learn a particular lesson in regard to this theme? Your work is not done once you have identified a theme. The real heart of your paper lies in your analysis and interpretation of a theme.

A few of the defining themes in *Frankenstein* include appearance versus reality, education, love, duty, and nature. Insanity and fears about insanity seem pervasive in the novel and play a large role in moving the plot forward. Other characters speculate broadly about Frankenstein's sanity, and Frankenstein repeatedly questions his own state of mind. One of the overwhelming fears of the novel is of being perceived as insane. Does insanity ever turn into a positive or liberating thing in this novel? Would all of the characters have been better off if Frankenstein had been suspected of insanity in the first place? Are all of the characters insane to some degree?

Of course, all of these fears and suspicions about insanity help to create the mood and shape the message of *Frankenstein*. The ways in which various characters perceive sanity and the workings of their own minds might be an even more important aspect of the novel's theme. Readers learn that characters are linked in several ways. Do characters get what they deserve? Does insanity explain or excuse some characters' behaviors?

Sample Topics:

1. **Education is more than just books and formal schooling:** What types of education do various characters receive, and what impact does education have on their lives?

   Frankenstein's formal schooling seems to have gone horribly wrong, though his self-education while creating the creature does not bode well either. The creature is entirely self-educated, and one could argue that he has a better understanding of the world than Frankenstein. How does Frankenstein describe his family's attitude toward education, and what impact does that have on events in the novel? In the creature's case, education leads to despair: "Increase of knowledge only discovered to me more clearly what a wretched outcast I was" (Shelley 156). Could those same words come from Frankenstein? The section of the novel in which the creature educates himself while hidden from the De Laceys was "condemned as wretchedly implausible, an objection made by almost all the reviewers" (Seymour 196). What did English people in the early nineteenth century believe about education, particularly self-education? How does this seem to influence Shelley's opinions in the novel?

2. **The importance/effects of nature:** Which characters are most affected by nature? How? Why? How does this make readers feel about those characters? Are we more connected to characters who are more connected to nature, for example?

Why does Shelley create these relationships with nature? Can we attribute all of this to her romantic background and/or sensibilities? Frankenstein says, "listen to my tale. I believe that the strange incidents connected with it will afford a view of nature, which may enlarge your faculties and understanding" (Shelley 58). Is this a reference to nature, as in the outdoors, or nature, as in human nature? Are the two always distinguishable from each other in the novel? Why would Shelley want to conflate human nature and Mother Nature? What effect does this have on our reading and understanding of the novel's characterizations? Nature is often soothing to Frankenstein: "The sight of the awful and majestic in nature had indeed always the effect of solemnizing my mind and causing me to forget the passing cares of life" (Shelley 120). The creature is also deeply affected and often soothed by nature: "The labours I endured were no longer to be alleviated by the bright sun or gentle breezes of spring" (Shelley 166). Is this the greatest similarity between the two characters? What conclusions about each character are we able to draw from their relationships with nature?

3. **Lessons from Frankenstein:** Frankenstein tells Walton, "Learn from me, if not by my precepts at least by my example, how dangerous is the acquirement of knowledge and how much happier that man is who believes his native town the world, than he who aspires to become greater than his nature will allow" (Shelley 76–77). What is the import of this utterance?

   Is this also Shelley's message to readers? How can we tell? Are we really supposed to learn from Frankenstein? Is the novel intended as a cautionary tale? Frankenstein tells Walton this before he begins the story of actually forming the creature, which foreshadows the impending doom. Is that the real intent of this warning—simply to set a tone? Can we argue that this is the main theme of the novel? How so? In what ways is this theme stronger than the others?

4. **Pursuit of knowledge:** Frankenstein asserts that "[a] human being in perfection ought always to preserve a calm and peaceful mind and never to allow passion or a transitory desire to disturb his tranquillity [sic]. I do not think that the pursuit of knowledge is any exception to this rule" (Shelley 79). What are the implications of this statement?

   Do we hear Shelley's voice coming through here? If so, where exactly is it? How can we tell? In what ways does this theme persist and develop throughout the novel? Are Frankenstein's beliefs here proved true through events in the book? In some ways, this philosophy works against the spirit of the age—the desire for knowledge, new ideas, and a certain air of rebellion. Does this seem to be Shelley's intention? How can we tell? Why would she put an important theme in the mouth of Frankenstein? Why is it so important to take into account the point of view from which these words come?

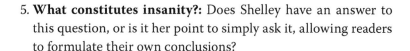

5. **What constitutes insanity?:** Does Shelley have an answer to
this question, or is it her point to simply ask it, allowing readers
to formulate their own conclusions?

Characters seem aware when they are on the brink or at least in
danger of being regarded as insane, and they address it directly:
"Remember, I am not recording the vision of a madman" (Shelley 76). This is Frankenstein speaking, yet the words might as
well come from Shelley herself. Is Shelley worried that readers
and reviewers will think she is insane? Is Frankenstein insane?
If so, does that excuse some of his thoughts and actions? What
about the creature? Might he also be insane or never really
mentally stable to begin with? Or are characters driven insane
by circumstances, behaviors, or one another? Frankenstein
does not share what he knows about the creature and William's
murder because he fears that people will regard his words as
"the ravings of delirium" (Shelley 102). Is this the same thing
as insanity? How so? Does his paranoia reveal the truth of
the suspicion? After Henry's death, Frankenstein begins tak-
ing laudanum and has several subconscious or semiconscious
experiences: "I maintained a continual silence concerning the
wretch I had created. I had a feeling that I should be supposed
mad, and this for ever chained my tongue" (Shelley 208). Is it
better to be actually insane or perceived as insane? Why are
the social perceptions so important, when Frankenstein feels
his life is virtually over anyway? Frankenstein is considering
events leading to Henry's death and considering what will
happen in the aftermath: "Recollection brought madness with
it. And when I thought of what had passed, a real insanity possessed me" (Shelley 213). Is this Shelley's definition of insanity? Is this Frankenstein's definition of insanity? What does it
mean when he says, "a real insanity"? Does that differentiate
it from "unreal" or a different kind of insanity? At the end of
the book, in one of the only observations of Frankenstein that
does not come from Frankenstein himself, Walton reports:
"Sometimes he commanded his countenance and tones and
related the most horrible incidents with a tranquil voice,

suppressing every mark of agitation—then, like a volcano bursting forth, his face would suddenly change to an expression of the wildest rage as he shrieked out his imprecations on his persecutor" (Shelley 231). How do we explain this behavior? Are these symptoms of insanity?

6. **Unfairness and inaccuracy in determining guilt and innocence:** Frankenstein reacts to William's murder: "Could he be (I shuddered at the conception) the murderer of my brother? No sooner did that idea cross my imagination than I became convinced of its truth. . . . He was the murderer! I could not doubt it. The mere presence of the idea was an irresistible proof of the fact" (Shelley 100–01).

   Should the creature be afforded the same "innocent until proven guilty" rights as people? Why or why not? Is Frankenstein jumping to conclusions, or, especially since we learn that he is in fact correct, does he possess some sort of superhuman connection or instinct? Are he and the creature so alike that they are in some way psychologically linked? Do they understand each other? Consider that habeus corpus was suspended in England during parts of the eighteenth and nineteenth centuries. Does that affect Shelley's views on guilt and innocence and when a person should be accused or imprisoned or punished for a crime? Is it ironic that the creature is not allowed the comforts or companionship of human nature, yet he is accused and rendered guilty as if he were a thinking, feeling human, rather than an animal who does not know better? Frankenstein feels considerable guilt eventually. Is it too little too late? Frankenstein thinks, "I was guiltless, but I had indeed drawn down a horrible curse upon my head, as mortal as that of crime" (Shelley 185). Is this true? Is he guiltless? And if so, is his "curse" the equivalent of an actual crime?

7. **The importance and fruitlessness of pity:** Who are we as readers supposed to feel sorry for? Do we pity the creature? Frankenstein? Both? Are we forced to choose between them?

Who does Shelley seem to be siding with? Frankenstein, after William's death, begins to feel remorse: "I suffered living torture. It was to be decided whether the result of my curiosity and lawless devices would cause the death of two of my fellow-beings" (Shelley 105). Does Frankenstein feel sorrier for himself than is justified? Does he behave as a victim or martyr, when really he is the instigator and the only one who can stop these horrifying things from happening? As the creature tries to convince Frankenstein to create his mate, he says, "tell me why I should pity man more than he pities me. . . . Shall I respect man when he contemns me? Let him live with me in the interchange of kindness, and, instead of injury, I would bestow every benefit upon him with tears of gratitude at his acceptance. But that cannot be; the human senses are insurmountable barriers to our union. But mine shall not be the submission of abject slavery" (Shelley 169). Do passages such as this one make us feel sorry for the creature? Why or why not? What seems to be Shelley's intention? How can we tell?

8. **The importance of solitude:** Why is it so important for Frankenstein and the creature to be alone?

Frankenstein ostracizes himself over his guilt for creating a creature that causes death and destruction: "[S]olitude was my only consolation—deep, dark, death-like solitude" (Shelley 114). Does this seem extreme or the reasonable reaction of someone involved the way Frankenstein is? Is solitude always a way of punishing oneself for action or inaction? Is solitude in this book constructed as a response to the "mob mentality" that had so recently ruled during the French Revolution? After Frankenstein dies, the creature laments: "'The fallen angel becomes a malignant devil. Yet he, even he, man's enemy, had friends and associates; I am quite alone'" (Shelley 243). Is solitude a desirable thing for Frankenstein and a misery for the creature? Is solitude only positive when it is associated with nature? Does solitude become dangerous for some characters?

9. **Compassion as the true indication of human nature:** Are compassion and sympathy different things? If so, how? In what ways does Frankenstein show compassion? In what ways does he show sympathy?

The creature asks Frankenstein to build him a mate, and Frankenstein recalls, "His words had a strange effect upon me. I compassionated him and sometimes felt a wish to console him; but when I looked on him, when I saw the filthy mass that moved and talked, my heart sickened, and my feelings were altered to those of horror and hatred. I tried to stifle them. I thought that, as I could not sympathize with him, I had no right to refuse him the small portion of happiness that I had it in my power to bestow" (Shelley 171). Does Frankenstein feel compassion for the creature? Or does he feel guilty because he cannot feel compassion for the creature, and is it this reaction that drives him to agree to create a mate? Does anyone show compassion toward Frankenstein? Does anyone feel sympathy for him? Which character(s) do you think Shelley wants readers to feel the most compassion or sympathy for? Why? How can you tell? After Frankenstein dies, the creature says, "I pitied Frankenstein and his bitter sufferings; my pity amounted to horror; I abhorred myself" (Shelley 242). What does this mean? Does the creature transfer his feelings for Frankenstein onto himself? Who truly deserves pity? Compassion?

10. **Dangers of selfishness:** Is Frankenstein inherently selfish? If he was more giving, more selfless, would a different ending to the book result?

As he creates the second creature, Frankenstein asks, "Had I any right for my own benefit to inflict this curse to everlasting generations?" (Shelley 189). Is he finally being responsible and unselfish here, or is this a continuation of his selfishness? Is Frankenstein's selfishness driving all of the action in the novel? Does Frankenstein look back at the end of his life, regretting that he did not see the selfishness of his actions? If he had known that Elizabeth would die, would he have acted differently and seen his refusal to comply with the creature as selfishness? Has Frankenstein become so wrapped up in his own tortures that he cannot even process that others might have feelings about him, about the situation, about something other than the creature? Is it the creature who is the most selfish of all? After Frankenstein dies, the creature says, "'A frightful selfishness hurried me on while my heart was torn with agony. Think ye that the groans of Clerval were music to my ear? My heart was made for love and sympathy'" (Shelley 241). Does this quotation suggest there are more similarities between Frankenstein and the creature than the narrative initially suggests?

Bibliography for Themes in *Frankenstein*

Forry, Steven Earl. *Hideous Progenies: Dramatizations of Frankenstein from Mary Shelley to the Present*. Philadelphia: U of Pennsylvania P, 1990. Print.

Fraistat, Neil and Steven E. Jones, eds. "Mary Wollstonecraft Shelley." *Romantic Circles*. 28 June 1999. Web. 26 May 2010.

Hitchcock, Susan Tyler. *Frankenstein: A Cultural History*. New York: W.W. Norton, 2007. Print.

Holmes, Richard. *The Age of Wonder: How the Romantic Generation Discovered the Beauty and Terror of Science*. New York: Vintage, 2008. Print.

Hoobler, Dorothy and Thomas Hoobler. *The Monsters: Mary Shelley and the Curse of Frankenstein*. New York: Little, Brown, 2006. Print.

The Journals of Mary Shelley, 1814–44. Paula R. Feldman and Diana Scott-Kilvert, eds. 2 vols. Oxford: Oxford UP, 1987. Print.

"Mary Wollstonecraft Shelley." *The Literature Network*. n.d. Web. 13 August 2010.

Mellor, Anne K. "Making a 'Monster': An Introduction to *Frankenstein*." *The Cambridge Companion to Mary Shelley*. Ed. Esther Schor. Cambridge: Cambridge UP, 2003. 9–25. Print.

———. *Mary Shelley: Her Life, Her Fiction, Her Monsters*. New York: Methuen, 1988. Print.

Moers, Ellen. *Literary Women*. Garden City, N.Y.: Doubleday, 1976. Print.

Morton, Timothy, ed. *Mary Shelley's Frankenstein: A Sourcebook.* London: Routledge, 2002. Print.

Pridmore, Jan. "Mary Shelley." *Literary History.* 17 April 2010. Web. 26 May 2010.

Robinson, Charles E., ed. *The Original Frankenstein: Mary Shelley's Earliest Draft and Percy Shelley's Revised Text.* 1816–1817. By Mary Wollstonecraft Shelley with Percy Bysshe Shelley. New York: Vintage, 2008. Print.

Schor, Esther, ed. *The Cambridge Companion to Mary Shelley.* Cambridge: Cambridge UP, 2003. Print.

Seymour, Miranda. *Mary Shelley.* New York: Grove Press, 2000. Print.

Shelley, Mary Wollstonecraft with Percy Bysshe Shelley. *Frankenstein; or, The Modern Prometheus.* The Original Two-Volume Novel of 1816–1817 from the Bodleian Library Manuscripts. Ed. Charles E. Robinson. New York: Vintage Books, 2008. Print.

Teuber, Andreas. "Mary Wollstonecraft Shelley." Brandeis University. n.d. Web. 13 August 2010.

Voller, Jack G. "Mary Shelley." *The Literary Gothic.* 27 April 2010. Web. 26 May 2010.

Woodbridge, Kim. "Mary Shelley and *Frankenstein.*" 2010. Web. 13 August 2010.

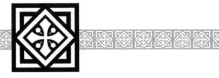

CHARACTERS IN
FRANKENSTEIN

READING TO WRITE

FRANKENSTEIN'S INTRODUCTION to his tale (told to Walton) includes an introduction to his family and friends:

From this time Elizabeth Lavenza became my playfellow, and, as we grew older, my friend. She was docile and good tempered, yet gay and playful as a summer insect. Although she was lively and animated, her feelings were strong and deep, and her disposition uncommonly affectionate. No one could better enjoy liberty, yet no one could submit with more grace than she did to constraint and caprice. Her imagination was luxuriant, yet her capability of application was great. Her person was the image of her mind; her hazel eyes, although as lively as a bird's, possessed an attractive softness. Her figure was light and airy; and, though capable of enduring great fatigue, she appeared the most fragile creature in the world. While I admired her understanding and fancy, I loved to tend on her, as I should on a favourite animal; and I never saw so much grace both of person and mind united to so little pretension. . . .

I was more calm and philosophical than my companion. Yet I was not so mild or yielding. My application was of longer endurance, but it was not so severe whilst it endured. I delighted in investigating the facts relating to the actual world—she busied herself in following the aerial creations of the poets. The world was to me a secret which I desired to discover—to her it was a vacancy which she sought to people with imaginations of her own.

> My brothers were considerably younger than myself, but I had a friend in one of my schoolfellows who compensated for this deficiency. Henry Clerval was the son of a merchant of Geneva, an intimate friend of my father. He was a boy of singular talent and fancy. I remember when he was only nine years old he wrote a fairy tale which was the delight and amazement of all his companions. His favourite study consisted in books of chivalry and romance; and, when very young, I can remember that we used to act plays composed by him out of these books, the principal characters of which were Orlando, Robin Hood, Amadis, and St. George. No youth could be more happy than mine. (Shelley 61–62)

What is *Frankenstein* conveying about Elizabeth? Does this characterization ring true throughout the book? Do we have reason to suspect (at this point in the book or later) that Frankenstein is giving us a biased view of Elizabeth, perhaps to predispose Walton (and, in Shelley's mind, readers) to hate the creature for killing her? What does "Her person was the image of her mind" mean exactly? Does it indicate the importance of possessing intelligence for women, as opposed to simply dutiful nature and beauty? Does Frankenstein (and Shelley) describe men differently from the way he describes women? If so, how? Why? If not, how does Shelley strike the balance, and why is it important? Do these characters sound too perfect, causing readers to be suspicious, to look for flaws? Do readers ever find such flaws? Why or why not? Provide examples. Is Frankenstein comparing Elizabeth to an animal when he says he "loved to tend on her, as I should on a favourite animal"? Did people in Shelley's time often refer to themselves or others as animals? What does this say about Frankenstein specifically and gender roles in general? The term *creature* was commonly used to describe or refer to humans, as Frankenstein uses it here, so it is likely that Shelley uses the term somewhat unconsciously when drawing characterizations and having characters refer to one another. Yet it draws distinct parallels between the creature and the humans referred to as creatures. Does Shelley seem to do this intentionally, given that she never gives the creature a particular name? Does Frankenstein imply a hierarchy, when comparing his own tendencies to Elizabeth's, perhaps that "practical" knowledge is better, more important, than poetical flights of fancy? Did Shelley believe this? How does this passage about Elizabeth's mind place the book squarely in the context of romanticism? Does Frankenstein imply that he would have been better off, perhaps not in his current life-and-death struggle, if he had paid more attention to poetry and been less devoted to "facts relating to the actual world"? What would have been different about their lives if Elizabeth had helped Frankenstein with the creature from the beginning?

What do we make of the description of Henry? Does it imply that Frankenstein is on some level in love with Henry? How so, or why not? Is Henry more similar to Elizabeth or to Frankenstein? Why is this important? What is the significance of the four figures Frankenstein mentions played roles in Henry's plays?

How does Shelley create moods around these characters, just from these brief, one-sided descriptions? How can we tell which characters she wants us to like, dislike, or disregard? Do any characters seem expendable? How so? How would these characterizations change if given from someone else's perspective? What would the creature, for example, say about Frankenstein? What would Elizabeth say about Henry?

STRATEGIES

Writing about characters in *Frankenstein* presents a wealth of options. The following suggestions serve as general methods for approaching these topics. Explore them as means of generating your own well-supported arguments and insights. Each of the topics discussed in this chapter could lead to a fruitful, original discussion of the novel.

Characters

When studying characters, there are several directions to take. You might look at character development, or what distinguishes one character from another. Elizabeth and Henry, for example, are similar in many ways. How does Shelley differentiate the two? You might also investigate change in a character, noting when a character seems to evolve (or devolve) in some way. How, for instance, does the creature change over the course of the novel? Does his general personality change, or does the world around him change? Or both? Along the same lines, you can choose to study a character who perhaps should change but does not. Frankenstein, for example, seems to remain purposefully ignorant in many ways. How does this explain his actions, and in what ways do readers (and some of the characters) wish he would change? Why?

It is always fascinating to study the ways in which a character is created. This requires you to look at specific words, phrases, settings, or moods that surround and help describe a character in order to see how Shelley helps readers form appropriate opinions of her characters.

Sample Topics:

1. **Victor Frankenstein:** How does Shelley want readers to feel about him, and how can we tell?

   Walton writes of him: "My affection for my guest increases every day. He excites at once my admiration and my pity to an astonishing degree. How can I see so noble a creature destroyed by misery without feeling the most poignant grief? He is so gentle, yet so wise; his mind is so cultivated; and when he speaks, although his words are culled with the choicest art, yet they flow with rapidity and unparalleled eloquence" (Shelley 56). Do readers feel the same way about Frankenstein? Why or why not? Does he begin to see himself and the creature as one and the same? Are his statements of remorse heartfelt? How can we tell? Is he suffering from some sort of depression or manic depressive illness? Where is the evidence of that? What seems to be Shelley's diagnosis or explanation? Would he be treated (medically or socially) differently now? How so? Why? Does Frankenstein have a death wish? Should Frankenstein sacrifice himself for the sake of others? Does the reader start to hope for Frankenstein's death? Why is the novel titled *Frankenstein*? Is it his story in a way that it is no one else's?

2. **The creature:** Is the creature believable as a character, as a physical specimen? As a thinking, feeling soul? Why doesn't the creature have a name?

   Is the creature like a young child? Is he like a foreigner in the land? Both? Neither? The creature says, "I am fearless and therefore powerful" (Shelley 191). Is this true? Is there anything that the creature is afraid of? Is he more powerful than Frankenstein? What do we make of the creature's reaction to a dead Frankenstein at the end?: "'That is also my victim. In his murder my crimes are consummate. Oh, Frankenstein! Generous and self-devoted creature, dare I ask thee to pardon me? I who destroyed thee by destroying those thou lovedst'" (Shelley 241). Why does the creature suddenly shoulder all responsibility? Does he deserve such a burden? Why or why not? Does the creature show more humility than Frankenstein? How does this change or reinforce readers' perceptions of the creature? Do we like him more or less at this point? Why? The creature asks, "when I destroyed his [Frankenstein's] hopes, I did not satisfy my own desires. . . . Still I desired love and fellowship, and I was still spurned. Was there no injustice in this? And am I the only criminal, while all mankind sinned against me?'" (Shelley 243). Is this the ultimate question in the book? Does this make readers sympathize with the creature, if we didn't before? Is his desire for companionship, a human necessity, what drives the entire book? Does the creature seem to be a man or a woman? How can we tell? Why is this important? In what ways would the novel change if the creature were the other gender?

3. **Robert Walton:** Is Walton an impartial observer, objectively reporting, or does he have a stake in all of this?

Does he seem to include all detail, or is he painting a particular picture for his sister? Why? As Frankenstein lay in delirious reflection on his life, Walton reports that he is "noble and godlike in ruin. He seems to feel his own worth and the greatness of his fall" (Shelley 233). Why does Walton idolize Frankenstein to such an extent? Does Frankenstein deserve such praise and lofty comparisons? Is there something about Walton's character that explains his hero-worship of Frankenstein? Is Walton's assessment of Frankenstein accurate? Why or why not? How can you tell? As Frankenstein dies, Walton laments, "Must I lose this admirable being? I have longed for a friend; I have sought one who would sympathize with and love me" (Shelley 233). Does this wish make Walton similar to the creature? If so, does that imply that all of humanity is similar to the creature in some way or that the creature contains an element of humanity that is pervasive? What are Walton's ambitions? Are they similar to Frankenstein in this regard?

4. **Elizabeth Lavenza:** Is she really a fully formed character, or is she just a type? How can we tell?

What are the effects of only seeing her from Frankenstein's point of view? Why is Elizabeth the only one willing to speak up for Justine? Should Elizabeth be pushier? What would Frankenstein have done if she had forced him to tell her all that he knew? Is Elizabeth sensitive to what is going on around her in ways that others are not? Does she seem to suspect Frankenstein's secret (or at least the fact that he has a secret) well before she learns that it exists? If so, why doesn't she do anything about it or push him harder to tell her? On their wedding day, she tells Frankenstein, "'Something whispers to me not to depend too much on the prospect which is opened before us, but I will not listen to such a sinister voice'" (Shelley 216). Does she have better instincts than Frankenstein? If he had had such premonitions, would he have even created the creature? Does Elizabeth's character help to illustrate gender differences in the novel? Does Shelley's perspective on gender roles seem progressive for her time? How does Elizabeth exemplify or refute nineteenth-century gender roles?

5. **The De Laceys:** Are they innocent, or are they representatives of the prejudices found in humanity?

Are the details of their background important, or are they simply representative types whose role in the plot could be filled by characters of varying backgrounds? Do we expect them to react differently to the creature? Why or why not? What do you suppose ultimately happens to the De Lacey family? Does this section of the novel seem realistic? Why or why not?

6. **Henry Clerval:** Why would Frankenstein, and Shelley, paint him without a single fault?

Why is it important to the plot that Henry dies? Is Henry in some ways the antithesis of Frankenstein? How would Henry have handled Frankenstein's situation differently if he were in Frankenstein's shoes? Why? How can you tell? Are Henry's sensibilities more romantic, or scientific? How can we tell? What would have happened if Henry had been involved with Frankenstein's creation from the beginning? Are we supposed to be upset when Henry dies, or is he an expendable character?

7. **Justine:** Is her death a noble one?

Should she have fought harder for herself? Why does Shelley tell us so much about her background? Does it explain her actions or somehow make us feel differently about her than we would otherwise given the information about her upbringing? Does she somehow represent the general role of women in the novel? How does class factor into the trial of Justine?

8. **William Frankenstein:** Why is it important that William is the first to die?

What are the most important facts about William—that he is just a child? That he is Frankenstein's youngest brother? In what ways do others' reactions to William's death influence our reading of and the events in the novel? William seems to have particular significance for Shelley. Her father's name was William, and had she been a boy, her name would have been William too. Shelley's son William was born on January 24, 1816, just a few months before Shelley began writing *Frankenstein*. Before beginning her work on *Frankenstein*,

Shelley had lost her first baby, a girl, and it affected her deeply: "She had grown up believing that her own birth had killed a woman brimming with vitality; to bear and rear a child was the best recompense she could offer to herself and to the Fates to whom her journal sometimes darkly alluded. Instead, she now bore the sense of a double murder; not only had she killed her mother but she had allowed her own baby girl to die. The fault, in both cases, was felt to be hers" (Seymour 130). Are these feelings of Shelley's similar to Frankenstein's feelings of guilt over William?

9. **A mate for the creature:** As he tries to convince Frankenstein to construct him a mate, the creature says, "What I ask of you is reasonable and moderate" (Shelley 170). Is it?

What is the ethical thing to do here? What would actually happen if Frankenstein complied with the request? Is there a greater chance that this second creature will turn out somehow worse than the first, because Frankenstein's attitude toward it is so decidedly negative? Think in terms of nature versus nurture. If this is the only point in their lives when Frankenstein expresses any sort of "parental" feeling or control in regard to the creature, how will it affect them?

Bibliography for Characters in *Frankenstein*

Forry, Steven Earl. *Hideous Progenies: Dramatizations of Frankenstein from Mary Shelley to the Present.* Philadelphia: U of Pennsylvania P, 1990. Print.

Fraistat, Neil and Steven E. Jones, eds. "Mary Wollstonecraft Shelley." *Romantic Circles.* 28 June 1999. Web. 26 May 2010.

Hitchcock, Susan Tyler. *Frankenstein: A Cultural History.* New York: W.W. Norton, 2007. Print.

Holmes, Richard. *The Age of Wonder: How the Romantic Generation Discovered the Beauty and Terror of Science.* New York: Vintage, 2008. Print.

Hoobler, Dorothy and Thomas Hoobler. *The Monsters: Mary Shelley and the Curse of Frankenstein.* New York: Little, Brown, 2006. Print.

The Journals of Mary Shelley, 1814–44. Paula R. Feldman and Diana Scott-Kilvert, eds. 2 vols. Oxford: Oxford UP, 1987. Print.

"Mary Wollstonecraft Shelley." *The Literature Network.* n.d. Web. 13 August 2010.

Mellor, Anne K. "Making a 'Monster': An Introduction to *Frankenstein.*" *The Cambridge Companion to Mary Shelley.* Ed. Esther Schor. Cambridge: Cambridge UP, 2003. 9–25. Print.

———. *Mary Shelley: Her Life, Her Fiction, Her Monsters.* New York: Methuen, 1988. Print.

Moers, Ellen. *Literary Women.* Garden City, N.Y.: Doubleday, 1976. Print.

Morton, Timothy, ed. *Mary Shelley's Frankenstein: A Sourcebook.* London: Routledge, 2002. Print.

Pridmore, Jan. "Mary Shelley." *Literary History.* 17 April 2010. Web. 26 May 2010.

Robinson, Charles E., ed. *The Original Frankenstein: Mary Shelley's Earliest Draft and Percy Shelley's Revised Text.* 1816–1817. By Mary Wollstonecraft Shelley with Percy Bysshe Shelley. New York: Vintage, 2008. Print.

Schor, Esther, ed. *The Cambridge Companion to Mary Shelley.* Cambridge: Cambridge UP, 2003. Print.

Seymour, Miranda. *Mary Shelley.* New York: Grove Press, 2000. Print.

Shelley, Mary Wollstonecraft with Percy Bysshe Shelley. *Frankenstein; or, The Modern Prometheus.* The Original Two-Volume Novel of 1816–1817 from the Bodleian Library Manuscripts. Ed. Charles E. Robinson. New York: Vintage Books, 2008. Print.

Teuber, Andreas. "Mary Wollstonecraft Shelley." Brandeis University. n.d. Web. 13 August 2010.

Voller, Jack G. "Mary Shelley." *The Literary Gothic.* 27 April 2010. Web. 26 May 2010.

Woodbridge, Kim. "Mary Shelley and *Frankenstein.*" 2010. Web. 13 August 2010.

FORM AND GENRE IN
FRANKENSTEIN

READING TO WRITE

FRANKENSTEIN IS marked by its chilling passages. This is one of the best-known passages in the novel, even in all of literature:

> I started from my sleep with horror, a cold dew covered my forehead, my teeth chattered, and every limb became convulsed, when, by the dim and yellow light of the moon as it forced its way through the window shutters, I beheld the wretch—the miserable monster whom I had created. He held up the curtain, and his eyes—if eyes they may be called—were fixed on me. His jaws opened, and he muttered some inarticulate sounds while a grin wrinkled his cheeks. He might have spoken, but I did not hear—one hand was stretched out to detain me, but I escaped and rushed down stairs. I took refuge in a court-yard belonging to the house which I inhabited, where I remained during the rest of the night, walking up and down in the greatest agitation, listening attentively, catching and fearing each sound as if it were to announce the arrival of the dæmonical corpse to which I had so miserably given life.
>
> Oh! no mortal could support the horror of that countenance. A mummy again endued with animation could not be so hideous as He. I had gazed on him while unfinished; he was ugly then. But when those muscles and joints were endued with motion, it became a thing such as even Dante could never have conceived. (Shelley 82)

This is one of Shelley's most effectively frightening passages. Why? What is it about the color yellow—the light of the moon as well as the color of the creature's eyes—that becomes so ominous? It comes up again after Frankenstein discovers Elizabeth dead on their wedding night: "I felt a kind of panic on seeing the pale yellow light of the moon illuminate the chamber" (Shelley 218). Why is the color yellow so often associated with the creature? In what ways does this scene inform readers that this is a scary book? A example of the horror genre?

Consider what makes this scene scary: the moon's light "forced its way" into the room, demonstrating an unusual level of violence already. The creature has already become a "wretch" and a "miserable monster," impressions that leave us in no doubt that Frankenstein has no affection for it and now considers it an adversary of sorts. Even the relatively simple words "if eyes they may be called" remind us that this is not a "regular" human being Shelley is describing, which makes it somewhat less predictable. Is the creature there to kill Frankenstein? What other details in this passage lead us to the fright that it creates?

STRATEGIES

The novel presents several compelling directions in exploring notions of form and genre. Shelley's work startles and endures in part because of the careful way she weaves together aspects of various genres. The suggestions presented here are in no way exhaustive and are meant to provide a jumping-off point rather than an answer key. Use these suggestions to find your own ideas and form your own analyses.

Form and Genre

Form and genre provide ways of classifying works that usually allow us to understand and study them more fully. Form is defined as the style and structure of a work, whereas genre is the type, or classification, of a work. Both form and genre are usually distinct from a work's content, though writers employ each specifically in order to convey a particular message, reach a certain audience, or to simply strengthen the impact of their work.

Sometimes gender, religion, race, or other factors can play a role in a writer's choices in regard to form and genre. Could a man have written

Frankenstein with similar results? Why or why not? What would be different? The same?

Sample Topics:

1. **Frame narrative:** What purposes do Walton's letters to his sister serve in the novel? What effect does the frame narrative have on readers?

A frame narrative is essentially a story within a story. It occurs when an introductory and concluding story is created for the purpose of containing another story, just as Walton's story "bookends" Frankenstein's. Why do we need Walton? When or how often do we forget that the story is being told to him? How does Shelley remind us of Walton's presence and role? Why does she do this? What does it add to the narrative? The story becomes cyclical in many ways. The creature implores Frankenstein to "Listen to my tale!" (Shelley 124). These are the same words that Frankenstein uses to Walton in the beginning, and they seem also to speak directly to readers. The creature is begging Frankenstein, with the same words, to listen, just as Frankenstein also begs Walton and Shelley begs her readers to listen. How does this technique help readers to feel involved in the various levels of the story?

2. **Letters and letter writing:** What would the book look like if it had been written today?

Letters from Walton to his sister are the vehicle for the entire story. Are they necessary? Could the story be told without them? Are they important beyond their role in relaying Frankenstein's story? Do letters in the novel have one particular role, or does each letter do something different for the structure and plot of the novel? Frankenstein writes a letter to Elizabeth when he is almost ready to tell her about the creature. Why does he not tell her in person? He writes: "I have one secret, Elizabeth, a dreadful one. It will chill your frame with horror; and then, far from being surprised at my misery, you will only wonder that I live. I will reveal this tale of misery and terror to you the day after our marriage" (Shelley 212). Would the story change in significant ways if told through cell phone calls, texts, or e-mails?

3. **Volume divisions:** How do the divisions between volumes change in various editions? Why?

Do Frankenstein and the creature get equal time in the novel? Why or why not? Is this important? Why? Why does Shelley break up the story into volumes at all? Why does she put the breaks in these particular places? What effect does this have on our reading?

4. **The supernatural:** How was the supernatural defined and expressed in Shelley's time? What supernatural elements do we recognize in the novel?

Using supernatural elements is part of the tradition of romantic literature. Shelley writes bluntly about this element in the novel. As Frankenstein decides to pursue his particular study of anatomy, he relates: "Unless I had been animated by an almost supernatural enthusiasm, my application to this study would have been irksome and almost intolerable" (Shelley 75). What other supernatural elements exist in the novel? Is the creature supernatural? Are Frankenstein's efforts, as well as his responses to their results, supernatural? What about the landscape? Frankenstein has limited experience with the supernatural: "In my education my father had taken the greatest precautions that my mind should be impressed by no supernatural horrors. I do not ever remember having trembled at a tale of superstition or to have feared the apparition of a spirit. Darkness had no effect upon my fancy; and a churchyard was to me merely as the receptacle of bodies deprived of life and which, from being the seat of beauty and strength, became food for the worm" (Shelley 75). Would the story have turned out differently if Frankenstein had been exposed to the supernatural throughout his life? Why or why not?

5. **Suspense:** What techniques does Shelley use to create suspense in the novel?

"Fear overcame me; I dared not advance, dreading a thousand nameless evils that made me tremble, although I was unable to define them" (Shelley 98–99). The evils are undefinable, which is potentially what makes them so threatening or scary. How does Shelley hint at what is going to happen, or at what has already happened? Consider what is perhaps the most memorable and chilling suspense-filled sentence of all: "I shall be with you on your marriage night" (Shelley 191). Does Shelley's breed of suspense prove effective when it comes to present-day readers? Why or why not?

6. **Science fiction:** In what ways does *Frankenstein* set the stage for the science fiction genre?

Frankenstein is often regarded as the first science fiction novel: "Mary's brilliance was to see that these weighty and often alarming ideas could be given highly suggestive, imaginative and even playful form. In a sense, she would treat male concepts in a female style. She would develop exactly what William Lawrence had dismissed in his lectures as 'hypothesis or fiction'. Indeed, it was to be an utterly new form of fiction— the science fiction novel" (Holmes 327). How is this novel different from other novels of Shelley's time? Is it significant that *Frankenstein* was written by a woman? Why or why not? Does Shelley seem aware that she is doing something new? How can you tell?

Bibliography for Form and Genre in *Frankenstein*

Forry, Steven Earl. *Hideous Progenies: Dramatizations of Frankenstein from Mary Shelley to the Present.* Philadelphia: U of Pennsylvania P, 1990. Print.

Fraistat, Neil and Steven E. Jones, eds. "Mary Wollstonecraft Shelley." *Romantic Circles*. 28 June 1999. Web. 26 May 2010.

Hitchcock, Susan Tyler. *Frankenstein: A Cultural History*. New York: W.W. Norton, 2007. Print.

Holmes, Richard. *The Age of Wonder: How the Romantic Generation Discovered the Beauty and Terror of Science*. New York: Vintage, 2008. Print.

Hoobler, Dorothy and Thomas Hoobler. *The Monsters: Mary Shelley and the Curse of Frankenstein*. New York: Little, Brown, 2006. Print.

The Journals of Mary Shelley, 1814–44. Paula R. Feldman and Diana Scott-Kilvert, eds. 2 vols. Oxford: Oxford UP, 1987. Print.

"Mary Wollstonecraft Shelley." *The Literature Network*. n.d. Web. 13 August 2010.

Mellor, Anne K. "Making a 'Monster': An Introduction to *Frankenstein*." *The Cambridge Companion to Mary Shelley*. Ed. Esther Schor. Cambridge: Cambridge UP, 2003. 9–25. Print.

———. *Mary Shelley: Her Life, Her Fiction, Her Monsters*. New York: Methuen, 1988. Print.

Moers, Ellen. *Literary Women*. Garden City, N.Y.: Doubleday, 1976. Print.

Morton, Timothy, ed. *Mary Shelley's Frankenstein: A Sourcebook*. London: Routledge, 2002. Print.

Pridmore, Jan. "Mary Shelley." *Literary History*. 17 April 2010. Web. 26 May 2010.

Robinson, Charles E., ed. *The Original Frankenstein: Mary Shelley's Earliest Draft and Percy Shelley's Revised Text*. 1816–1817. By Mary Wollstonecraft Shelley with Percy Bysshe Shelley. New York: Vintage, 2008. Print.

Schor, Esther, ed. *The Cambridge Companion to Mary Shelley*. Cambridge: Cambridge UP, 2003. Print.

Seymour, Miranda. *Mary Shelley*. New York: Grove Press, 2000. Print.

Shelley, Mary Wollstonecraft with Percy Bysshe Shelley. *Frankenstein; or, The Modern Prometheus*. The Original Two-Volume Novel of 1816–1817 from the Bodleian Library Manuscripts. Ed. Charles E. Robinson. New York: Vintage Books, 2008. Print.

Teuber, Andreas. "Mary Wollstonecraft Shelley." Brandeis University. n.d. Web. 13 August 2010.

Voller, Jack G. "Mary Shelley." *The Literary Gothic*. 27 April 2010. Web. 26 May 2010.

Woodbridge, Kim. "Mary Shelley and *Frankenstein*." 2010. Web. 13 August 2010.

LANGUAGE, SYMBOLS, AND IMAGERY IN *FRANKENSTEIN*

READING TO WRITE

S HELLEY'S PORTRAYAL of the creature's awakening is much more subtle and calm, in some ways, than the mad scientist's manic cries of
"It's alive!" that we remember from film versions. She sets the stage deliberately and completely, to have the full effect on readers:

> It was on a dreary night of November that I beheld my man completed;
> with an anxiety that almost amounted to agony, I collected instruments
> of life around me that I might infuse a spark of being into the lifeless
> thing that lay at my feet. It was already one in the morning, the rain
> pattered dismally against the window panes, and my candle was nearly
> burnt out, when by the glimmer of the half-extinguished light I saw the
> dull yellow eye of the creature open. It breathed hard, and a convulsive
> motion agitated its limbs.
>
> How can I describe my emotion at this catastrophe, or how delin-
> eate the wretch whom with such infinite pains and care I had endea-
> voured to form? His limbs were in proportion, and I had selected his
> features as beautiful. Beautiful!—Great God! His yellow skin scarcely
> covered the work of muscles and arteries beneath; his hair was of a lus-
> trous black and flowing; and his teeth of a pearly whiteness; but these
> luxuriances [sic] only formed a more horrid contrast with his watery
> eyes, that seemed almost of the same colour as the dun white sockets in

which they were set, his shriveled complexion, and straight black lips.
(Shelley 80–81)

Why are the details of setting so important? Dreary November, night, one o'clock, rainy, candle nearly extinguished: What do these specific references add to the mood? What sort of tone is set through this use of detail?

Why does Frankenstein immediately use the word *catastrophe*? Frankenstein almost begins to seem like a loving parent, constructing his creation with "care" and calling it "beautiful." But then the word *beautiful* becomes ironic and menacing. How? Why? Why does the color yellow become so significantly associated with physical descriptions of the creature?

How has the imagery of the creature changed from Shelley's description to the green, stiff-legged monster with bolts in his neck that has dominated pop cultural representation?

Why do the creature's eyes, complexion, and lips overwhelm his physical appearance and deflect attention from his lovely hair and teeth? What vision do we get from the description "watery eyes"? Is the creature on the verge of crying? What sort of aura do those two words create around the creature? Somehow we begin to see the creature as sad or frightening, never as delighted or friendly. What is it about the description of the eyes that can suggest that interpretation or reaction? Why is Frankenstein immediately horrified? He confesses: "I had worked hard for nearly two years for the sole purpose of infusing life into an inanimate body. For this I had deprived myself of rest and health. I had desired it with an ardour that far exceeded moderation; but, now that I had succeeded, these dreams vanished, and breathless horror and disgust filled my heart" (Shelley 81). The creature is not even off the laboratory table yet. It has not done anything wrong yet, so Frankenstein is not disgusted by its crimes against himself or humanity in general. So is it something purely physical, something only about the creature's appearance that disturbs Frankenstein to this degree? It's hard to overstate the importance of this particular moment in the novel. If Frankenstein had responded differently to the creature immediately after seeing it come to life, what might have changed about subsequent events in the book? Is it fair to say that everything that happens from this point on in the book stems from Frankenstein's initial negative reaction to the creature's appearance? What message is Shelley conveying to readers, if this is the case?

STRATEGIES

Language, symbols, and imagery are key building blocks in any work of literature. Recurring motifs, objects, actions, and references serve as potential indicators of an author's intentions and present any number of viable essay topics. Use the suggestions as a starting point to map out your own original discussion of a particular aspect of *Frankenstein*'s verbal and visual realms.

Language, Symbols, and Imagery

Writing about the language, symbols, and imagery contained in a novel requires you to look specifically at how the work is constructed, as opposed to just studying its content. Pay particular attention to words, phrases, ideas, and their repetition in order to begin to see how Shelley uses language, symbols, and imagery. Summarizing the content may be necessary for illustrating particular points, but it is not the desired goal of this type of essay. You will want to look at elements such as syntax, word choice, and diction. Do some characters speak differently from others? If so, why? Speech can be tied to a variety of central issues, such as economic class, education, geography, and stress, just to name a few. Discovering that two characters have distinct ways of speaking might lead you to research their economic classes and respective educations, requiring some background in the novel's historical context. Ultimately, you are looking at Shelley's choices as a writer and suggesting and analyzing possible reasons for such choices.

Finding symbolism in a work involves looking for an element or aspect that stands for something else. Is a letter just a letter in *Frankenstein,* or might a letter stand for a character's honor, the machinations of society, or the necessity of clear communication? What kinds of things seem to be important to the novel and its characters? These things might be tangible objects such as letters or particular foods, but they might also be something such as a particular color associated with similar qualities, traits, or emotions throughout the book.

Imagery encapsulates things that can be perceived with our five senses. Shelley was a master of imagery, which partially explains why *Frankenstein* is so often adapted into plays, movies, and television series. Are there elements of imagery that recur throughout the novel, perhaps associated with specific characters, places, or activities? For example, is it always dark and dreary around a certain character, offering a clue to this character's disposition, lifestyle, or the ways in which Shelley is asking us to perceive this character?

Sample Topics:

1. **Point of view:** Why do we only get Frankenstein's, Walton's, and the creature's points of view? How significant is it that we only hear the creature's point of view secondhand?

   We hear from Walton, Frankenstein, and the creature (though only then as Frankenstein recounts the creature's tale to Walton). What do we learn about Frankenstein? How does he reveal his own character, for better or worse? We see some characters (his father, Henry, William, Elizabeth) only through Frankenstein's point of view. How does that affect their characterization? Do they seem less developed because he only recognizes or discusses certain aspects of them, so we do not get to see them as "whole" or fully realized people? Do they seem less realistic, too perfect? Why is it important and significant that we see them in this way, rather than hearing from them directly? Why is it important that we get to experience (at least on some level) the creature's point of view? Walton's? Can we trust that Frankenstein is telling the creature's story accurately? Why or why not? How can we tell? What might be his motivations for changing the creature's tale?

2. **Foreshadowing:** What does the foreshadowing add to the novel? What would the novel be like without it?

   Frankenstein recalls: "I had an obscure feeling that all was not over and that he would still commit some signal crime which by its enormity would almost efface the recollection of the past" (Shelley 115). Does this build suspense, even though we know, because of the structure of the book, that Frankenstein and the creature are both still alive at this point?

3. **Light:** Is light always presented in contrast to dark?

Frankenstein's realization of how to animate the human body is relayed as "[a] light so brilliant and wondrous yet so simple" (Shelley 75–76). We know that this description carries a sense of foreboding at least for those familiar with the outcome of the story. Does this mean that Shelley intended the image of light to contain suggestions and connotations of wrong, despair, grief, things usually associated with darkness? Does darkness ever become a good or positive thing? What does Frankenstein assume about himself and his world when he recalls that "life and death appeared to [him] ideal bounds, which [he] should first break through, and pour a torrent of light into our dark world" (Shelley 78). Now Frankenstein sees himself as in charge of this light—in control—right as he is remembering creating the creature. Does light mean the opposite—positive associations—to the creature? The creature remembers, "Soon a gentle light stole over the heavens and gave me a sensation of pleasure" (Shelley 129). Frankenstein seems to be suffering from depression or some sort of manic disorder, but it is often cast in terms of light and darkness: "my melancholy, which every now and then would return by fits and, with a devouring blackness, overcast the approaching sunshine" (Shelley 174). How does light affect characters differently? What do these effects reveal about each character?

4. **Narration:** Why does most of the story come from Frankenstein? Why is Walton's role so important?

Frankenstein talks directly to Walton and thus, by extension, the readers: "I see by your eagerness and the wonder and hope which your eyes express, my friend, that you expect to be informed of the secret with which I am acquainted—that cannot be. Listen patiently to the end of my story, and you will easily perceive why I am reserved upon that subject. I will not lead you on, unguarded and ardent as I then was, to your destruction and infallible misery" (Shelley 76). What effect does this have on us as readers? What were Shelley's intentions by adopting this method of storytelling? Does it take us out of the course of the plot or draw us in more deeply?

5. **Simile:** In what ways does Shelley use simile to make larger points?

Shelley writes, "[M]en appear to me as monsters thirsting for each other's blood" (116). Interesting that this image invokes the vampire of John Polidori's work, *The Vampyre,* begun in the same time and place as *Frankenstein.* If men are now monsters, to which men does Elizabeth refer? Or is it Shelley referring to the men of her own time and country? Is this her response to revolutionary activities or to the beginnings of the Industrial Revolution? Is it a gendered comment, remarking on the useless bloodthirst of men, as opposed to the gentler, more productive ways of women? Are there particular men in the novel to whom Elizabeth is or might be referring? Who are they, and why are they so violent toward one another? Does it change the meaning of the statement to realize that Elizabeth speaks it, rather than Frankenstein, or even the creature?

6. **Questions:** Which characters ask questions most often? How is this significant? Does Shelley intend for them (or for readers) to answer these questions? How can you tell?

Characters often ask questions of themselves, of others, but almost always of the reader: "Why did you form a monster so hideous that even you turned from me in disgust?" (Shelley 155). The questions remain largely unanswered in the text. Does Shelley seem to be doing this on purpose? Is it a reflection of the cliché about life, that it holds more questions than answers? Is Shelley asking these questions of readers too?

Does this strategy make us feel sorry for the creature with all of his questions and essentially take his side in the argument? These questions raise others. For example, does a man like Frankenstein truly deserve companionship and happiness after what he has done (or has not done), and does the creature truly deserve to be miserable and alone? All three "narrators" (Frankenstein, the creature, and Walton) use this technique.

7. **Seasons:** Do the seasons hold significance other than the standard "spring means renewal, winter means death" symbolism?

The seasons play an important role in the novel's setting: The creature comes to life on a dreary November night, spends the summer and fall with the De Laceys in relative harmony and contentment, and in the dark, cold, brutal winter, the creature and Frankenstein hunt each other to their deaths. Why is Shelley so deliberate and straightforward about time frames and seasons, as well as aspects of weather? The creature tells Walton: "'Some years ago, when the images this world affords first opened on me, when I felt the cheering warmth of summer and heard the rustling of leaves and the chirping of birds—and these were all to me—I should have wept to die; and now it is my only consolation'" (Shelley 244). It is worth noting that it is in the deepest winter, in the iciest place on earth, when both the creature and Frankenstein are destroyed.

8. **Irony:** Does Frankenstein ever truly realize or understand the similarities between himself and the creature?

After Elizabeth dies, Frankenstein thinks, "A fiend had snatched from me every hope of future happiness. No creature had ever been so miserable as I was; so frightful an event was single upon earth" (Shelley 220). These words could just as easily have come from the creature itself. Does Shelley seem to be drawing these parallels, creating such irony on purpose? Why? How can you tell?

Bibliography for Language, Symbols, and Imagery in *Frankenstein*

Forry, Steven Earl. *Hideous Progenies: Dramatizations of Frankenstein from Mary Shelley to the Present.* Philadelphia: U of Pennsylvania P, 1990. Print.

Fraistat, Neil and Steven E. Jones, eds. "Mary Wollstonecraft Shelley." *Romantic Circles.* 28 June 1999. Web. 26 May 2010.

Hitchcock, Susan Tyler. *Frankenstein: A Cultural History.* New York: W.W. Norton, 2007. Print.

Holmes, Richard. *The Age of Wonder: How the Romantic Generation Discovered the Beauty and Terror of Science.* New York: Vintage, 2008. Print.

Hoobler, Dorothy and Thomas Hoobler. *The Monsters: Mary Shelley and the Curse of Frankenstein.* New York: Little, Brown, 2006. Print.

The Journals of Mary Shelley, 1814–44. Paula R. Feldman and Diana Scott-Kilvert, eds. 2 vols. Oxford: Oxford UP, 1987. Print.

"Mary Wollstonecraft Shelley." *The Literature Network.* n.d. Web. 13 August 2010.

Mellor, Anne K. "Making a 'Monster': An Introduction to *Frankenstein.*" *The Cambridge Companion to Mary Shelley.* Ed. Esther Schor. Cambridge: Cambridge UP, 2003. 9–25. Print.

———. *Mary Shelley: Her Life, Her Fiction, Her Monsters.* New York: Methuen, 1988. Print.

Moers, Ellen. *Literary Women.* Garden City, N.Y.: Doubleday, 1976. Print.

Morton, Timothy, ed. *Mary Shelley's Frankenstein: A Sourcebook.* London: Routledge, 2002. Print.

Pridmore, Jan. "Mary Shelley." *Literary History.* 17 April 2010. Web. 26 May 2010.

Robinson, Charles E., ed. *The Original Frankenstein: Mary Shelley's Earliest Draft and Percy Shelley's Revised Text.* 1816–1817. By Mary Wollstonecraft Shelley with Percy Bysshe Shelley. New York: Vintage, 2008. Print.

Schor, Esther, ed. *The Cambridge Companion to Mary Shelley.* Cambridge: Cambridge UP, 2003. Print.

Seymour, Miranda. *Mary Shelley.* New York: Grove Press, 2000. Print.

Shelley, Mary Wollstonecraft with Percy Bysshe Shelley. *Frankenstein; or, The Modern Prometheus.* The Original Two-Volume Novel of 1816–1817 from the Bodleian Library Manuscripts. Ed. Charles E. Robinson. New York: Vintage Books, 2008. Print.

Teuber, Andreas. "Mary Wollstonecraft Shelley." Brandeis University. n.d. Web. 13 August 2010.

Voller, Jack G. "Mary Shelley." *The Literary Gothic.* 27 April 2010. Web. 26 May 2010.

Woodbridge, Kim. "Mary Shelley and *Frankenstein.*" 2010. Web. 13 August 2010.

HISTORY AND
CONTEXT IN
FRANKENSTEIN

READING TO WRITE

WE CONTINUE to learn about Frankenstein's background as he tells Walton his life story:

> When I had attained the age of seventeen, my parents resolved that I should become a student at the University of Ingolstadt. I had hitherto attended the schools of Geneva, but my father thought it necessary for the completion of my education that I should be made acquainted with other customs than those of my native country. My departure was therefore fixed at an early date. But before the day resolved upon could arrive, the first misfortune of my life occurred: an omen, as it were, of my future misery.
>
> Elizabeth had caught the scarlet fever; but her illness was not severe, and she quickly recovered. During her confinement, many arguments had been urged to persuade my mother to refrain from attending upon her. She had yielded to our entreaties; but, when she heard that her favourite was recovering, she could no longer debar herself from her society and entered her sick chamber long before the danger of infection was past. The consequences of this imprudence were fatal: on the third day my mother sickened. Her fever was malignant, and the looks of her attendants prognosticated the worst evil. On her death-bed the fortitude and benignity of this admirable woman did not desert her.

She joined the hands of Elizabeth and myself. "My children," said she, "it was on your union that my firmest hopes of future happiness were placed. It will not be the consolation of your father. Elizabeth, my love, supply my place to your young cousins. Alas! I regret that I am taken from you; and, happy and beloved as I am, is it not hard to quit you all? But these are not thoughts befitting me; I will endeavour to resign myself cheerfully to death and will indulge a hope of meeting you in another world."

Was it common at the turn of the nineteenth century for Europeans to send young adults to other countries, to "be made acquainted with other customs"? What does this detail reveal about the Frankenstein family, its sensibilities, its ideology, its definitions of education and life-long learning? What does such an education produce for Frankenstein? Does he take full advantage of such opportunities? Why or why not? Is Frankenstein's mother's death really an omen of what is to come, or is it simply bad luck? Does Frankenstein use his mother's death as an excuse for his future actions? Does Frankenstein's mother's death reflect Shelley's own mother's death in any way? How common was it for people, particularly women, to die so young? What generally became of families with relatively young children when the mother died? How common was scarlet fever in Shelley's lifetime or in the late eighteenth century (the time frame of the book)? Was it more common for women to die of such a disease than for men? Is this because women spent more time nursing the ill? What were the medical understandings of the time? What kinds of "cures" and treatments for scarlet fever existed and were commonly employed? How did treatments differ depending on class? Does Elizabeth survive the fever because the family has enough money for proper medical treatment? Does this passage demonstrate Elizabeth's and Frankenstein's mother's roles as "typical" women of their time? How so, or why not? What were common ways of dealing with dying, death, and burial in Shelley's time? What are the religious sentiments implied in Frankenstein's mother's final speech? In what ways is this passage an illustration of parenting styles of the time? In what ways are the Frankensteins atypical in their parenting? How do these parenting styles influence Frankenstein's views and treatment of his creature?

STRATEGIES

No author writes independent of his or her times. The historical context enters or shapes the work in some way. The following suggestions present various possible topics for writing about the history and context of *Frankenstein* as well as general methods for approaching these topics.

Researching and consulting reference sources is one way of bolstering an argument that grapples with a work's contexts and historical influences.

History and Context

Part of the early nineteenth-century world that we now take for granted comes from Shelley's novel. She describes and comments on the world around her in creative and mesmerizing ways. While certainly her work is still largely fictional, it is grounded in some of the complexities of life in preindustrial England.

Studying history and context always involves research, and you can begin by choosing a character, scene, theme, or setting from the novel and inquiring as to whether that is what things were really like. Be aware that sometimes the time period in which the action of the book takes place can be different from the time in which the book was written and published, and even a few years can make a difference. Once you have determined the similarities and differences between the real world of the times and the one Shelley creates, you can begin to speculate about what Shelley is trying to convey through her portrayal.

History and context might also pertain to the author's biography. Consider the ways in which Shelley's own background may have contributed to *Frankenstein*. Are there details about Shelley's life or beliefs that add depth and understanding to our reading of this novel?

Sample Topics:

1. **Prometheus:** The full title of the novel is: *Frankenstein, or The Modern Prometheus*. What bearing does the subtitle have on the novel?

   Prometheus is part of a Greek myth, first written down by Aeschylus: "Prometheus tricks Zeus into choosing a sacrifice of bones wrapped in fat, leaving for humans fine meat hidden inside organs . . . then he . . . gives the valuable gift of fire to humans. As punishment Zeus straps Prometheus to a barren rock, above earth yet below heaven, and sends his eagle every night to feed on the Titan's" liver (Hitchcock 52). Does this tale bear any resemblance to *Frankenstein*? How so? Search for more complete accounts of Prometheus to make more accurate comparisons. Aeschylus wrote the tragedy in three parts: *Prometheus Bound, Prometheus the Fire-Bringer,* and *Prometheus Unbound,* though "only the first survived in its entirety" (Hitchcock 52). After *Frankenstein* was published, Percy Bysshe Shelley wrote *Prometheus Unbound,* "a lyrical drama promising a total renovation of nature and human experience, symbolized by the release of the Titan from the rock" (Hitchcock 52). Why were the Shelleys (as well as other romantics and Victorians) so interested in the Prometheus myth?

2. **Frankenstein's conception:** The story of Shelley's inspiration for the novel is almost as legendary as the novel itself. In what ways does the novel's background become an important part of the tale, in terms of its place in literary history?

The Shelleys (not yet married) spent the summer of 1816, which "was proving to be the worst in living memory for England and Western Europe," with their baby son, William, and friends John Polidori, Lord Byron, and Claire Clairmont on Lake Geneva in Switzerland (Seymour 151).

In Percy Shelley's preface to the 1818 edition, he writes:

> this story was begun in the majestic region where the scene is principally laid, and in society which cannot cease to be regretted. I passed the summer of 1816 in the environs of Geneva. The season was cold and rainy, and in the evenings we crowded around a blazing wood fire, and occasionally amused ourselves with some German stories of ghosts, which happened to fall into our hands. These tales excited in us a playful desire of imi-

tation. Two other friends (a tale from the pen of one of whom would be far more acceptable to the public than any thing I can ever hope to produce) and myself agreed to write each a story, founded on some supernatural occurrence. . . . The following tale is the only one which has been completed. (Robinson 433)

How does this excerpt set the stage for the tale of *Frankenstein*? Does the story within the novel become confused with the story about the novel's conception? Where? Why?

3. **Scientists:** What seems to be Shelley's overall message about science and its practitioners? Are her opinions fair? How can you tell?

Shelley never uses the word *scientist,* because it had not yet been coined. She writes of "natural philosophers" instead. The coming Industrial Revolution was helping to find uses for science—steam engines, factories, medicine, for example—so that the creativity and wonder inherent to science seemed, to some, gone. Does the novel convey or support protests against this new practical application of science? Which kind and era of science does Frankenstein's creation belong to? Is it different depending on whether you are talking about Frankenstein's intent or his actual results or the way he responds to the results? Shelley biographer Miranda Seymour offers insight into the science behind the novel: "Bath was well supplied with libraries, offering . . . Humphrey Davy's lucid accounts of chemical experiments for her to work into Victor Frankenstein's scientific education. (Mary did not feel entirely at ease in this field; one of the surprises of *Frankenstein* is its paucity of scientific detail)" (173). Do these facts change the way we read the book? Why or why not? We might also consider the opinion that "in Victor Frankenstein . . . [Shelley] had created a composite figure who in many ways was typical of a whole generation of scientific men. The shades of 'inflammable' Priestley, the deeply eccentric Cavendish, the ambitious young Davy, the sinister Aldini and the glamorous, iconoclastic William Lawrence may all have contributed something to the portrait" (Holmes 328). Who are these other scientists? Does knowing more about them add to our knowledge and understanding of Frankenstein and the novel as a whole?

4. **The sublime:** Can this entire novel be called sublime in some ways? Is the creature itself sublime?

The sublime is inexplicable and often overwhelming. It cannot be measured or calculated, and the romantics loved to write about it. The most famous example from *Frankenstein* is the great storm:

> we witnessed a violent and terrible thunderstorm. . . . [T]he thunder burst at once with frightful loudness from various quarters of the heavens. I remained while the storm lasted, watching its progress with curiosity and delight. As I stood at the door, on a sudden I beheld a stream of fire issue from an old and beautiful oak about twenty yards from our house; and so soon as the dazzling light vanished, the oak had disappeared, and nothing remained but a blasted stump. When we visited it the next morning, we found the tree shattered in a singular manner. It was not splintered by the shock, but entirely reduced to thin ribbands of wood. I never saw any thing so utterly destroyed. The catastrophe of the tree excited my extreme astonishment. (Shelley 65)

What effect does this storm have on the rest of the novel? Where else in the novel are there examples of the sublime? How do the instances describing the sublime influence the plot and action or characters' thoughts? Compare Mary Shelley's descriptions of nature and the sublime with Percy Shelley's treatment of the same in poems such as "Mont Blanc."

5. **Jagged, icy landscape:** What is so significant about this particular setting?

Why does Shelley choose such dramatic, extreme settings in the novel, especially for encounters between Frankenstein and the creature? Polar expeditions like Walton's were going on at the time Shelley wrote the novel. How much of what she writes about is real? What effect would such realities have had on her contemporary readers? Why? In what ways does Shelley experience such extreme environments in her own life?

6. **Illness:** What types of maladies are considered illness? What is the distinction between illness and insanity?

Why is Frankenstein so prone to illness? He seems to have a weak constitution. Was this an accepted fact of the time, that such emotional and mental distress would naturally create a weakness of body as well? Or does it have more to do with the creature? Perhaps the creature is somehow draining Frankenstein of life, as if they are really one person functioning with one body, mind, spirit, and soul. Is illness in the novel a reflection of reality, or is it a metaphor?

7. **Class system:** What would change about the situation in the novel if Justine had not been a servant?

Frankenstein explains to Walton that "[a] servant at Geneva does not mean the same thing as a servant in France or England—Justine was thus received into our family to learn the duties of a servant, which in our fortunate country does not include a sacrifice of the dignity of a human being" (Shelley 89). Is this true of Geneva in the late eighteenth century? Was the opposite true of France and England at this time? Is Shelley making a particular statement here, as an English woman herself? What if the necklace had been found in Elizabeth's pocket? What would change about the situation if Justine had not been treated like a member of the family? Is her status as a servant part of the reason that Frankenstein does virtually nothing to help her? Is Frankenstein simply exaggerating about his family's magnanimity?

8. **Politics and power struggles:** In what ways does the novel reflect political power struggles of Shelley's time?

The creature asks Frankenstein,

> "Do you dare destroy my hopes?"
>
> "Begone," I replied; "I do break my promise; never will I create another like yourself, equal in deformity and wickedness."
>
> "Slave," said the wretch, "I before reasoned with you, but you have proved yourself unworthy of my condescension. Remember that I have power; you believe yourself miserable, but I can make you so wretched that the light of day will be hateful to you. You are my creator, but I am your master—Obey!"
>
> "Wretch," said I, "the hour of my weakness is past, and the period of your power is arrived. Your threats cannot move me to do an act of wickedness, but they confirm in me a resolution of not creating you a companion in vice. Shall I in cold blood set loose upon the earth a dæmon whose delight is in death and wretchedness? Begone! I am firm, and your words will only exasperate my rage." (Shelley 190)

Consider the late eighteenth-century French Revolution, when the citizens began questioning and then dismantling the absolute monarchy, claiming misuse of power. Is Shelley commenting on such events in this novel? Given her parents and background, she potentially equates this imbalance of power to gender inequality, each side wanting the other to obey and conform, without understanding, compassion, or anyone truly listening. Does Shelley seem to be saying that some people should be more powerful than others, or is she advocating something closer to equality? Why? How can you tell?

9. **Slavery:** In what ways does the relationship between Frankenstein and the creature become a metaphor for slavery?

Who is the slave, and who is the master in this novel? Biographer Miranda Seymour writes that Shelley's "creature,

Frankenstein's electrically charged child, would remind her
readers of the danger and wickedness of their attitude to the
people whose unpaid labour sweetened their coffee. The 1814
Treaty of Paris secured French trading rights in slavery for
an additional five years; the main characters of Mary's novel
are all of French origin. Only the creature, "assembled from
whatever limbs can be got, is made as rootless as a trans-
ported slave. Judged . . . by his appearance and not by his acts,
the Creature becomes an unprincipled monster" (162–63).
Both Mary and Percy Shelley refused to use sugar, as a stand
against the slavery that produced it. Does *Frankenstein* in
some ways read as a treatise against slavery? Why or why not?
Would Shelley's contemporary readers have recognized the
slavery issues in the novel? What was the general response to
such commentary? Why?

10. **Shelley's ideas:** What does Shelley really believe? How can we
tell?

In Percy Bysshe Shelley's preface to the 1818 edition, he writes,
"The opinions which naturally spring from the character and
situation of the hero are by no means to be conceived as exist-
ing always in [her] own conviction; nor is any inference justly
to be drawn from the following pages as prejudicing any philosophical doctrine of whatever kind" (Robinson 433). Study
Mary Wollstonecraft Shelley's biography and other writings.
Does this statement by Percy appear to be true? Is it simply
Shelley's way of protecting herself (or Percy protecting her)
from criticism and presuppositions about her life and beliefs?

Bibliography for History and Context in *Frankenstein*

Forry, Steven Earl. *Hideous Progenies: Dramatizations of Frankenstein from
Mary Shelley to the Present.* Philadelphia: U of Pennsylvania P, 1990. Print.
Fraistat, Neil and Steven E. Jones, eds. "Mary Wollstonecraft Shelley." *Romantic
Circles.* 28 June 1999. Web. 26 May 2010.
Hitchcock, Susan Tyler. *Frankenstein: A Cultural History.* New York: W.W. Nor-
ton, 2007. Print.

Holmes, Richard. *The Age of Wonder: How the Romantic Generation Discovered the Beauty and Terror of Science.* New York: Vintage, 2008. Print.

Hoobler, Dorothy and Thomas Hoobler. *The Monsters: Mary Shelley and the Curse of Frankenstein.* New York: Little, Brown, 2006. Print.

The Journals of Mary Shelley, 1814–44. Paula R. Feldman and Diana Scott-Kilvert, eds. 2 vols. Oxford: Oxford UP, 1987. Print.

"Mary Wollstonecraft Shelley." *The Literature Network.* n.d. Web. 13 August 2010.

Mellor, Anne K. "Making a 'Monster': An Introduction to *Frankenstein*." *The Cambridge Companion to Mary Shelley.* Ed. Esther Schor. Cambridge: Cambridge UP, 2003. 9–25. Print.

———. *Mary Shelley: Her Life, Her Fiction, Her Monsters.* New York: Methuen, 1988. Print.

Moers, Ellen. *Literary Women.* Garden City, NY: Doubleday, 1976. Print.

Morton, Timothy, ed. *Mary Shelley's Frankenstein: A Sourcebook.* London: Routledge, 2002. Print.

Pridmore, Jan. "Mary Shelley." *Literary History.* 17 April 2010. Web. 26 May 2010.

Robinson, Charles E., ed. *The Original Frankenstein: Mary Shelley's Earliest Draft and Percy Shelley's Revised Text.* 1816–1817. By Mary Wollstonecraft Shelley with Percy Bysshe Shelley. New York: Vintage, 2008. Print.

Schor, Esther, ed. *The Cambridge Companion to Mary Shelley.* Cambridge: Cambridge UP, 2003. Print.

Seymour, Miranda. *Mary Shelley.* New York: Grove Press, 2000. Print.

Shelley, Mary Wollstonecraft with Percy Bysshe Shelley. *Frankenstein; or, The Modern Prometheus.* The Original Two-Volume Novel of 1816–1817 from the Bodleian Library Manuscripts. Ed. Charles E. Robinson. New York: Vintage Books, 2008. Print.

Teuber, Andreas. "Mary Wollstonecraft Shelley." *Brandeis University.* n.d. Web. 13 August 2010.

Voller, Jack G. "Mary Shelley." *The Literary Gothic.* 27 April 2010. Web. 26 May 2010.

Woodbridge, Kim. "Mary Shelley and *Frankenstein*." 2010. Web. 13 August 2010.

PHILOSOPHY
AND IDEAS IN
FRANKENSTEIN

READING TO WRITE

A T THE end of his life, Frankenstein tells Walton:

"When younger . . . I felt as if I was destined for some great enterprise. My feelings are profound, but I possessed a coolness of judgement [sic] that fitted me for illustrious achievements. This sentiment of the worth of my nature supported me when others would have sunk, for I deemed it criminal to throw away in useless grief those talents that might be useful to my fellow-creatures. When I reflected on the work that I had completed, no less a one than the creation of a sensitive and rational animal, I could not rank myself with the herd of common projectors. But this feeling which supported me now serves only to plunge me lower in the dust. All my speculations and hopes are as nothing; and, like the Archangel who aspired to omnipotence, I am chained in an eternal hell. My imagination was vivid, yet my powers of application were intense—by the union of these qualities I conceived the idea and executed the creation of a man. Even not I cannot recollect without passion my reveries while the work was incomplete—I trod heaven in my thoughts—now exulting in my powers—now burning with the idea of their consequences. From my infancy I was imbued with high hopes and a lofty ambition, but how am I sunk! Oh my friend! if you had known me as I once was, you would not recognize me in this state of degradation. Despondency rarely visited my heart; a high destiny seemed to bear me on—until I fell, oh! never, never again to rise." (Shelley 233)

What is a "common projector," and why does Frankenstein not want to associate himself with such a category? To what does Frankenstein refer when he speaks of "throw[ing] away in useless grief those talents that might be useful to my fellow-creatures"? Is he talking about his talents as an animator of life? Is he talking about the aftermath of William's death? Is he simply determined to not have any regrets on his deathbed? Should he have regrets? If so, what should they be? If not, why not? Does Frankenstein, on some level, still believe that he did a great thing by creating the creature? Is this true? Why or why not? How would other characters, including the creature, answer this question? Is it accurate and fair for Frankenstein to compare himself with an archangel? Why or why not? Has Frankenstein ever truly considered the consequences of his actions? What evidence is there of this? Are there two Frankensteins here—one early in the book and a completely different one at the end? How do we compare the two? Why is it important to recognize both of them? On the other hand, can it be argued that Frankenstein does not change enough throughout the course of the book, that he should have grown and changed and learned more than he does—or at least more than he can articulate or admit? This is the only place in the novel, after the creature becomes animated, that Frankenstein refers to it as "man" rather than creature, monster, or another derogatory term. Does this mean that Frankenstein now recognizes the humanity of the creature, even the similarities between him and his creation?

STRATEGIES

The realm of philosophy and the abstract notions and ideas it centers on play a prominent role in the novel. The following suggestions are intended to stimulate thinking about the philosophical notions that Shelley addressed and that influenced and found their way into her novel. The discussions and the questions posed are not intended to be a specific blueprint for an essay but a starting point for your own explorations, interpretations, and inquiries.

Philosophy and Ideas

Writing about the philosophy and ideas found in a text is similar to writing about the text's theme, except that philosophy and ideas are applied more generally and can be located, in some sense, outside the text as well. When writing about a book's philosophy, you are looking for the ways in which the work comments on general ideas. Murder, for example, is a strong element in this novel, begging readers to pursue the ethics and myriad questions behind the action. Is there such a thing as a "philosophy of murder" or a rationale behind murder? Was this true in the early nineteenth century? Could people avoid conviction, for example, by pleading manslaughter instead of murder? Were there "degrees" of murder then as there are now (first-degree murder versus second-degree murder)? How are such degrees and decisions considered aspects of philosophical inquiry rather than simply innate parts of our understanding?

Sample Topics:

1. **Playing God:** What is Shelley asking her readers to think about, in terms of human beings imagining themselves as powerful as God? Is there a message about Christianity here, or is the point actually about human nature rather than religion?

Frankenstein laments, "A new existence would bless me as its creator and source; many happy and excellent natures would owe their being to me. No father could claim the gratitude of this child so completely as I should deserve theirs. Pursuing these reflections, I thought that if I could bestow animation upon lifeless matter I might in process of time (although I now found it impossible) renew life where death had apparently devoted the body to corruption" (Shelley 78). Are we supposed to understand that he is overreaching, or are we supposed to side with him, caught up in the possibilities of creation without thinking of the consequences and parallels with Christian beliefs? The creature takes Frankenstein to task: "All men hate the wretched—how then must I be hated who am miserable beyond all living things. Yet you, my creator, hate me and spurn me, thy creature, to whom thou are bound with ties only dissoluble by the death of one of us. You purpose to kill me. How dare you sport thus with life? Do your duty towards me, and I will do mine towards you and the rest of mankind" (Shelley 122). Do we sympathize with the creature here? Has Frankenstein really gone too far? Is the creature in control at all? Is he handing over control to Frankenstein, or has Frankenstein been in control all along? How can we tell?

2. **Religion:** Does this novel work if you disregard the Christian messages or aspects? If a non-Christian reads it, does it have the same effect that it would have on someone perhaps more familiar with the Christian ideology?

We see briefly the story of Safie and her Muslim background, learning that her mother "taught her to aspire to higher powers of intellect and an independence of spirit forbidden to the female followers of Mahomet" (Shelley 149). Is this about religion, or is this a gender issue, or both? At the end, Frankenstein believes that he is compelled to destroy the creature by a higher power, something beyond him: "[T]he vengeance that burned within me died in my heart, and I pursued my path towards the destruction of the dæmon more as a task enjoined by heaven, as the mechanical impulse of some power of which I was unconscious, than the ardent desire of my soul" (Shelley 227). Is this Frankenstein's way of absolving himself of guilt? Later Frankenstein asks, "Oh! when will my guiding spirit, in conducting me to him, allow me the rest I so much desire?" (Shelley 231). Is his guiding spirit good or evil? Why? How can you tell?

3. **Destiny:** What is left up to fate, religion, and nature, and what is decided by characters and their actions?

After Frankenstein speaks with Waldman about the wonders of modern science, just before he begins creating his creature, he thinks, "Thus ended a day memorable to me, for it decided my destiny" (Shelley 73). Does this place blame for the ensuing catastrophes on Waldman? Would events in Frankenstein's life have been the same without this conversation with Waldman? Is Frankenstein alleviating his own guilt by not claiming responsibility for his actions? What is the destiny of the creature? Is destiny given/created by God or by man, and does the creature's circumstance blur that line in a new way? Does Frankenstein author the creature's destiny through his response (or lack thereof) to him once he comes alive? Is Frankenstein really "destined" to endure this? Couldn't he stop it if he chose to? Is Shelley using the word indiscriminately, or is it purposeful, to convey messages about destiny, inevitability, and the lack of free will? The creature happens upon the Frankenstein family and kills William. Is this destiny, chance, divine intervention, coincidence? How can we explain the irony here, that, of all people he could have happened on in his travels, this family is the one? Is Frankenstein's destiny ever truly fulfilled? He dies before the creature is actually destroyed, and we do not actually know for certain that the creature dies in the end. Is this Frankenstein's destiny or simply his selfish wish for vengeance and closure?

4. **Dedication to science:** Does science really advance more rapidly than other disciplines?

Shelley writes, "None but those who have experienced it can conceive of the enticements of science. In other studies you go as far as others have gone before you, and there is nothing more to know; but in a scientific pursuit there is continual food for discovery and wonder" (74). Is this something that Shelley seems to believe, too, or just Frankenstein? What does this statement reveal about Frankenstein and perhaps the lopsidedness of his dedications or priorities in life? Is this the general view of science at the time?

5. **Forgiveness:** Does Shelley seem to have a particular message about forgiveness? If so, what is it?

Frankenstein's father seems perpetually calm and reasonable: "Come, Victor, not brooding with thoughts of vengeance against the assassin, but with feelings of peace and gentleness that will heal instead of festering the wound of our minds" (Shelley 97). What would happen if Frankenstein chose to forgive the creature for his actions against William and Justine? What would happen if the creature chose to forgive Frankenstein for shunning him, rejecting him? Do characters who choose vengeance always do the wrong thing? Are their actions and motives ever understandable? With whom do we sympathize most in this regard?

6. **Importance of truth:** What is truth exactly?

Elizabeth asks, "when falsehood can look so like the truth, who can assure themselves of certain happiness?" (Shelley 117). Is happiness completely wrapped up in truth? What happens to happiness when a person lies or is lied to? Is this a warning, of sorts, to Frankenstein from Elizabeth, revealing her suspicion that he has not told her the absolute truth? Is honesty always the best policy in this novel? Can we argue that Shelley has a particular message about honesty and truth in this novel? If so, what is it? Frankenstein writes a letter to Elizabeth in which he tells her that he has a secret, "a dreadful one" that he will only tell her on the day after their wedding. Is this fair? Why is it important to be completely truthful only after they are married?

7. **Nature of man:** What exactly is the difference between human and beast, human and creature?

Shelley writes, "Alas! why does man boast of sensibilities above those apparent in the brute; it only renders them more necessary beings. If our impulses were confined to hunger, thirst, and desire, we might be nearly free; but now we are moved by every wind that blows and by every chance word or scene that that wind may convey to us" (121). If this is what constitutes the human, then where does the creature fit? Can he be defined by this description, or is he merely a beast? Is Frankenstein eventually reduced to the status of an animal, living only to sate his "hunger, thirst, and desire" for revenge?

8. **Importance (danger) of self-reflection:** Which characters are able to reflect honestly about themselves? Why?

Which characters are unable to see themselves truthfully or unwilling to even examine themselves? Why? What effect does this have on their lives? On the plot? The creature has tremendous powers of self-reflection: "As I read, however, I applied myself much personally to my own feelings and condition. . . . What did this mean? Who was I? What was I? Whence did I come? What was my destination? These questions continually recurred, but I was unable to solve them" (Shelley 153). Does this make the creature more intelligent or superior to others? Why or why not? How so? What is Shelley's message here?

9. **What is freedom?** What message about this concept does Shelley convey? Was she responding to the political realities of her day?

Frankenstein thinks, "If he [the creature] were vanquished, I should be a free man. Alas! what a freedom—such as the peasant endures when his family have been massacred before his eyes, his cottage burnt, his lands laid waste, and he is turned adrift, homeless pennyless, and alone—but free. Such would be my liberty" (Shelley 211). How does the creature define freedom? Or does he even have a concept of it? Can a person be physically, politically free and yet imprisoned by one's own mind? Is this part of Shelley's message, perhaps even her warning, about too much knowledge or the misuse of knowledge, creating prisons and even madness that an actual prison can never replicate? Is she advocating for some kind of revolution that others recoil from, for fear of imprisonment? Is she saying that these freedoms are lures worth pushing out of one's own head?

Bibliography for Philosophy and Ideas in *Frankenstein*

Forry, Steven Earl. *Hideous Progenies: Dramatizations of Frankenstein from Mary Shelley to the Present*. Philadelphia: University of Pennsylvania P, 1990. Print.

Fraistat, Neil and Steven E. Jones, eds. "Mary Wollstonecraft Shelley." *Romantic Circles*. 28 June 1999. Web. 26 May 2010.

Hitchcock, Susan Tyler. *Frankenstein: A Cultural History*. New York: W.W. Norton, 2007. Print.

Holmes, Richard. *The Age of Wonder: How the Romantic Generation Discovered the Beauty and Terror of Science*. New York: Vintage, 2008. Print.

Hoobler, Dorothy and Thomas Hoobler. *The Monsters: Mary Shelley and the Curse of Frankenstein*. New York: Little, Brown, 2006. Print.

The Journals of Mary Shelley, 1814–44. Paula R. Feldman and Diana Scott-Kilvert, eds. 2 vols. Oxford: Oxford UP, 1987. Print.

"Mary Wollstonecraft Shelley." *The Literature Network*. n.d. Web. 13 August 2010.

Mellor, Anne K. "Making a 'Monster': An Introduction to *Frankenstein*." *The Cambridge Companion to Mary Shelley*. Ed. Esther Schor. Cambridge: Cambridge UP, 2003. 9–25. Print.

———. *Mary Shelley: Her Life, Her Fiction, Her Monsters*. New York: Methuen, 1988. Print.

Moers, Ellen. *Literary Women*. Garden City, N.Y.: Doubleday, 1976. Print.

Morton, Timothy, ed. *Mary Shelley's Frankenstein: A Sourcebook*. London: Routledge, 2002. Print.

Pridmore, Jan. "Mary Shelley." *Literary History*. 17 April 2010. Web. 26 May 2010.

Robinson, Charles E., ed. *The Original Frankenstein: Mary Shelley's Earliest Draft and Percy Shelley's Revised Text*. 1816–1817. By Mary Wollstonecraft Shelley with Percy Bysshe Shelley. New York: Vintage, 2008. Print.

Schor, Esther, ed. *The Cambridge Companion to Mary Shelley*. Cambridge: Cambridge UP, 2003. Print.

Seymour, Miranda. *Mary Shelley*. New York: Grove Press, 2000. Print.

Shelley, Mary Wollstonecraft with Percy Bysshe Shelley. *Frankenstein; or, The Modern Prometheus*. The Original Two-Volume Novel of 1816–1817 from the Bodleian Library Manuscripts. Ed. Charles E. Robinson. New York: Vintage Books, 2008. Print.

Teuber, Andreas. "Mary Wollstonecraft Shelley." Brandeis University. n.d. Web. 13 August 2010.

Voller, Jack G. "Mary Shelley." *The Literary Gothic*. 27 April 2010. Web. 26 May 2010.

Woodbridge, Kim. "Mary Shelley and *Frankenstein*." 2010. Web. 13 August 2010.

COMPARISON AND CONTRAST IN *FRANKENSTEIN*

READING TO WRITE

THE MOST obvious opportunity for writing comparison and contrast essays about *Frankenstein* is the study of Victor Frankenstein and the creature. One of several passages where this becomes evident is Frankenstein's conversation with the magistrate:

As I spoke, rage sparkled in my eyes. The magistrate was intimidated; "You are mistaken," said he, "I will exert myself; and if it is in my power to seize the monster, be assured that he shall suffer punishment proportionate to his crimes. But I fear from what you have yourself described to be his properties that this will prove impracticable and that, while every proper measure is pursued, you should endeavour to make up your mind to a disappointment."

"That cannot be," said I wildly. "But all that I can say will be of little avail. My revenge is of no moment to you; yet, while I allow it to be a vice, I confess that it is the devouring and only passion of my soul; my rage is unspeakable when I reflect that the murderer whom I have turned loose upon society still exists. You refuse my just demand. I have but one resource, and I devote myself either in my life or death to his destruction." I trembled with excess of agitation as I said this; there was frenzy in my manner and something, I doubt not, of that haughty fierceness which the martyrs of old were said to have possessed. But to a Genevese magistrate, whose mind was occupied by far other ideas than those of devotion and heroism, this elevation of mind had much the appearance of madness. He endeavoured to soothe me as a nurse does a child, and reverted to my tale as the effects of delirium. "Man," I cried, "how ignorant art thou in thy pride of wisdom! Cease; you know not what it is you say." (Shelley 223)

Is Frankenstein a martyr? Is the creature? Are either of them victims? Is there a clear protagonist and antagonist in the novel, or do they become too conflated to distinguish clearly? How can we compare the magistrate's reaction to learning about the creature to what Frankenstein imagined all through the book would happen if he told anyone? Does this make readers frustrated with the authorities? With Frankenstein? Is Frankenstein acting like a snob when he says the magistrate is too preoccupied to fully grasp the importance of heroism and the difference between madness and whatever could be described as happening to Frankenstein—devotion, single-mindedness? Is he, in fact, insane and simply unable to recognize it in himself? Are his acts heroic? If so, are they heroic throughout the book, or is this a turning point where he becomes the hero he should have been all along? Or is the opposite true, that Frankenstein has been a hero all along and this is the turning point at which he becomes a villain? Is the creature the real hero in the novel? How so? Why? Does Frankenstein imagine himself a hero and this is in fact what causes his ultimate downfall? Does he simply drive himself insane, or is he driven insane by the creature? Are they both driven to madness by society's refusal to believe or accept them? Perhaps the female victims are the true heroes, only partially informed of what is happening and why but willing and able to suffer the consequences anyway. If the magistrate is treating Frankenstein like a child, is it possible that Frankenstein is acting like a child at this point? Could those words that Frankenstein speaks to the magistrate at the end of this passage have just as easily and accurately been said to Frankenstein? What is "pride of wisdom" and who has more of it—the magistrate, Frankenstein, or the creature?

It is important to remember when writing a comparison or contrast paper that listing similarities and differences is not enough. You need to find a clear focus, a reason for conveying your argument to your readers, so that your examples for comparison and/or contrast support a larger point.

STRATEGIES

A novel with such a long and rich legacy as *Frankenstein* presents a wealth of opportunities for comparison and contrast essays. Topics can explore elements or concerns contained within the work or reach beyond the novel to an adaptation or other work of literature or cultural output. All the topics discussed in this chapter could turn into effective essays or pave the way to a stronger topic of your own formulation.

Comparison and Contrast

Writing a paper that compares and contrasts elements of the novel involves much more than simply listing similarities and differences between two or more things. These lists might help you early in the drafting process, but your paper eventually needs to go beyond these more simplistic points and observations to discuss why these similarities or differences are notable and important to the novel. You would do well to ask questions such as: Does Shelley intentionally set up some comparisons in order to perhaps show different points of view or circumstances? Do we notice particular comparisons and contrasts simply because of the time in which we live that have shaped and influenced our perceptions of the early nineteenth century?

One of the most interesting things you can do with this type of paper is to make a comparison between two or more things/characters that on the surface seem highly similar. The more surprising your comparison or contrast is, the more engaging your paper could be to your readers (provided you back up your argument with sufficient evidence from the text). You cannot make a comparison or contrast statement based solely on your own perceptions and feelings about the work. Whatever claim you decide to make must be supportable through the text itself.

Sample Topics:

1. **Frankenstein at the beginning, Frankenstein at the end:** Does he change? Too much? Not enough? Does he learn anything? Too much? Not enough?

How do readers feel about Frankenstein at the beginning of the book? At the end? In what way does he change or not change? At the end, Frankenstein tells Walton: "Think not, Walton, that in the last moments of my existence I feel that burning hatred and ardent desire of revenge that I once expressed; but I feel myself justified in desiring the monster's death. During these last days I have been occupied in examining my past conduct; nor do I find it blameable [sic]. In a fit of enthusiastic madness, I created a rational creature and was bound towards him to assure, as far as in me lay, his happiness and well-being. This was my duty, but there was one still paramount to this. My duties towards my fellow-creatures had greater claims because they included a greater portion of happiness or misery" (Shelley 239). Did Frankenstein fail in all respects, never showing the creature any hint of this "duty" he now feels so strongly? Is he right to have no regrets? Does it seem evident that he has learned something?

2. **The creature and Frankenstein:** Is Frankenstein a hypocrite for regarding the creature as a monster? Is Frankenstein also larger than life in some ways?

Are both the creature and Frankenstein created as human, only to be regarded as monsters because of their choices and actions? Does Frankenstein's soul in some way transfer to the creature? Frankenstein describes the creature as "forced to destroy all who were dear to me" (Shelley 101). The phrase *forced to destroy* implies that the creature has no choice. Or does it simply mean that Frankenstein's part in all of this, if it is in fact his spirit wrapped up in the creature's actions, is involuntary? Are they alter egos? Are they one and the same, sharing a mind and body? Both refer to their "relationship" with the other as some form of slavery. Why so extreme? Both claim to be "persecuted and tortured" (Shelley 202). Are they? One more than the other? Is one a victim and one a martyr? Neither? After Frankenstein dies, the creature says, "'Once my fancy was soothed by dreams of virtue, of fame, and of enjoyment. . . . I cannot believe that I am he whose thoughts were once filled with sublime and transcendant [sic] visions of loveliness. . . . The fallen angel becomes a malignant devil'" (Shelley 243). If we did not know who spoke these words, would we be able to tell if they came from the creature or Frankenstein? Do the two characters become completely interchangeable by the end of the novel?

3. **Walton and Frankenstein:** Is Walton similar to Frankenstein in fundamental ways? Are they both more similar to the creature than they might like to admit?

Walton says of Frankenstein: "I begin to love him as a brother; and his constant and deep grief fills me with sympathy and compassion. He must have been a noble creature in his better days, being even now in wreck so attractive and amiable" (Shelley 55). Why does Walton like, even love, Frankenstein so quickly? Why does he trust him? Does this mean that readers should trust Frankenstein too? Does it reveal something about Walton's character? Walton calls Frankenstein *creature*, which of course later becomes one of the words most frequently used to describe Frankenstein's creation.

4. **Name calling:** Frankenstein and the creature call each other a variety of names. What do the two lists reveal?

Frankenstein says that he "began the creation of a human being" but never again refers to it as such (Shelley 77). He calls his manufactured progeny dæmon, creature, wretch, dæmoniacal corpse, "a thing such as even Dante could never have conceived" (Shelley 82), hideous guest, monster, spectre, animal, fiend, devil, vile insect, my persecutor, villain, hideous enemy, my adversary, and man (only once, p. 233). The creature calls Frankenstein: "my natural master and king" (Shelley 123), creator, Cursed Creator (Shelley 155), tyrant, tormentor, slave, "my last victim" (Shelley 242). Are either of them more accurately describing themselves when they choose to label each other with these names? How important is the context of each instance when Frankenstein and the creature refer to each other?

5. **Science and nature:** Which characters represent or seem to follow the path of science, and which represent or seem to follow the path of nature? Why? How can we tell?

How are science and nature defined during Shelley's lifetime? What do her uses of these disciplines or categories reveal about her ideology and beliefs? Frankenstein says of Elizabeth: "I delighted in investigating the facts relating to the actual world— she busied herself in following the aerial creations of the poets. The world was to me a secret which I desired to discover—to her it was a vacancy which she sought to people with imaginations of her own" (Shelley 62). Are science and nature always at odds with each other in the novel? Do they ever work in harmony?

6. **Revisions and versions of the novel:** Why was this novel so often and so substantially revised?

There are several versions of *Frankenstein*. Two were printed in Shelley's lifetime: the original 1818 version as well as the heavily revised 1831 edition. We also have Shelley's original version, as well as Percy Bysshe Shelley's edits to that version. Mary Shelley's original is about 170 pages; with Percy Shelley's changes, it is about 200 pages. How important is it to consider *Frankenstein* a co-authored project? Mary Shelley's biographer, Miranda Seymour, writes: "Collaboration on a project adds 'zest and vivacity', Mary wrote many years later. She, in 1816, was the writer, putting down her daily composition in good plain language which Percy Shelley worked over to produce an imposing rhetorical flourish. Their readings and discussions were joint" (172–73). What did the novel gain from all of these changes through the years? What did it lose? Which version should be most commonly read? Why? Which version would Shelley most approve?

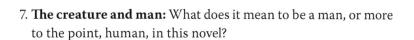

7. **The creature and man:** What does it mean to be a man, or more to the point, human, in this novel?

Walton writes, "Oh! be men, or be more than men; be steady to your purposes and firm as rock. This ice is not made of such stuff as your hearts might be; it is mutable and cannot withstand you, if you say that it shall not. Do not return to your families with the stigma of disgrace marked on your brows; return as heroes who have fought and conquered and who know not what it is to turn their backs on the foe" (Shelley 237). Is this what the creature has been doing all along? Is he, in fact, "more than men" in all kinds of different ways? Which characters in the book behave according to these precepts set out by Walton? Does this reveal anything about Shelley's perceptions of humanity or, more specifically, manliness?

Bibliography for Comparison and Contrast in *Frankenstein*

Forry, Steven Earl. *Hideous Progenies: Dramatizations of Frankenstein from Mary Shelley to the Present.* Philadelphia: U of Pennsylvania P, 1990. Print.

Fraistat, Neil and Steven E. Jones, eds. "Mary Wollstonecraft Shelley." *Romantic Circles.* 28 June 1999. Web. 26 May 2010.

Hitchcock, Susan Tyler. *Frankenstein: A Cultural History.* New York: W.W. Norton, 2007. Print.

Holmes, Richard. *The Age of Wonder: How the Romantic Generation Discovered the Beauty and Terror of Science.* New York: Vintage, 2008. Print.

Hoobler, Dorothy and Thomas Hoobler. *The Monsters: Mary Shelley and the Curse of Frankenstein.* New York: Little, Brown, 2006. Print.

The Journals of Mary Shelley, 1814–44. Paula R. Feldman and Diana Scott-Kilvert, eds. 2 vols. Oxford: Oxford UP, 1987. Print.

"Mary Wollstonecraft Shelley." *The Literature Network.* n.d. Web. 13 August 2010.

Mellor, Anne K. "Making a 'Monster': An Introduction to *Frankenstein*." *The Cambridge Companion to Mary Shelley.* Ed. Esther Schor. Cambridge: Cambridge UP, 2003. 9–25. Print.

———. *Mary Shelley: Her Life, Her Fiction, Her Monsters.* New York: Methuen, 1988. Print.

Moers, Ellen. *Literary Women.* Garden City, N.Y.: Doubleday, 1976. Print.

Morton, Timothy, ed. *Mary Shelley's Frankenstein: A Sourcebook.* London: Routledge, 2002. Print.

Pridmore, Jan. "Mary Shelley." *Literary History.* 17 April 2010. Web. 26 May 2010.

Robinson, Charles E., ed. *The Original Frankenstein: Mary Shelley's Earliest Draft and Percy Shelley's Revised Text.* 1816–1817. By Mary Wollstonecraft Shelley with Percy Bysshe Shelley. New York: Vintage, 2008. Print.

Schor, Esther, ed. *The Cambridge Companion to Mary Shelley.* Cambridge: Cambridge UP, 2003. Print.

Seymour, Miranda. *Mary Shelley.* New York: Grove Press, 2000. Print.

Shelley, Mary Wollstonecraft with Percy Bysshe Shelley. *Frankenstein; or, The Modern Prometheus.* The Original Two-Volume Novel of 1816–1817 from the Bodleian Library Manuscripts. Ed. Charles E. Robinson. New York: Vintage Books, 2008. Print.

Teuber, Andreas. "Mary Wollstonecraft Shelley." Brandeis University. n.d. Web. 13 August 2010.

Voller, Jack G. "Mary Shelley." *The Literary Gothic.* 27 April 2010. Web. 26 May 2010.

Woodbridge, Kim. "Mary Shelley and *Frankenstein.*" 2010. Web. 13 August 2010.

INDEX